Flowise AI, 2nd Edition

A Developer's Guide to Building LLM Applications, RAG Systems, and Agentic Workflows

Written By
Maxime Lane

Flowise AI, 2nd Edition
*A Developer's Guide to Building LLM Applications, RAG Systems, and
Agentic Workflows*

Copyright © 2025 Maxime Lane. All rights reserved.

Table of Content

Preface

A. About the Second Edition

Welcome to the second edition of *Flowise AI: A Developer's Guide to Building LLM Applications, RAG Systems, and Agentic Workflows*. This new edition represents a significant evolution from the original release, reflecting both the rapid advancements in AI technologies and the invaluable feedback received from our community of developers and practitioners.

In this updated edition, I've taken a comprehensive look at the latest developments in large language models (LLMs), retrieval-augmented generation (RAG) systems, and the design of agentic workflows. I've expanded on foundational topics while introducing new chapters that dive deep into advanced integrations, performance optimization, and modern deployment strategies. My goal is to ensure that you not only understand the technical concepts but also appreciate their practical applications in today's fast-paced AI landscape.

Key improvements include:

- **Expanded Content:** In-depth coverage of new AI models and frameworks that have emerged since the first edition, along with updated best practices.
- **Enhanced Practical Examples:** Refined code snippets, real-world case studies, and interactive exercises that bridge theory and practice.
- **Improved Structure:** A more intuitive flow of content with clearer chapter transitions, detailed sub-sections, and additional summaries to reinforce key concepts.
- **Community-Driven Enhancements:** Incorporation of feedback and contributions from the growing Flowise AI community, ensuring the content is both relevant and reflective of real-world challenges.
- **Future-Proof Insights:** Discussions on emerging trends, future directions, and how developers can continue to evolve alongside the rapidly changing AI ecosystem.

This edition is designed to serve as a comprehensive guide that is accessible to both newcomers and seasoned developers. Whether you are setting up your first workflow or fine-tuning advanced agentic systems, this book aims to empower you with the tools, knowledge, and insights needed to innovate and excel in the dynamic world of AI.

B. What's New and Improved

In this second edition, I've reimagined *Flowise AI* to better meet the evolving needs of developers and AI practitioners. Here are the key enhancements and updates you can expect:

- **Expanded Coverage of Advanced Technologies:**
  I dive deeper into state-of-the-art large language models (LLMs) and introduce the latest advancements in retrieval-augmented generation (RAG) systems. This includes updates on model architectures, fine-tuning techniques, and integration strategies that reflect current industry trends.
- **Enhanced Agentic Workflow Design:**
  Recognizing the growing importance of autonomous systems, I've enriched our discussion on agentic workflows. The new content details advanced multi-agent coordination, improved communication protocols between agents, and optimized approaches for parallel processing. Real-world case studies and interactive examples illustrate how these workflows can be scaled and adapted in complex environments.
- **Improved Practical Examples and Code Walkthroughs:**
  I've updated and expanded our code samples to cover a broader range of use cases, from building intelligent chatbots to designing custom RAG systems. The examples have been refined to be more accessible, with step-by-step explanations that bridge the gap between theory and implementation.
- **Modernized Deployment and Integration Strategies:**
  With the rapid evolution of cloud services and containerization technologies, this edition includes updated guides for local and cloud-based deployments. New sections cover best practices for container orchestration with Docker and Kubernetes, CI/CD integration, and managing scalable AI workflows in production environments.
- **Optimized Performance and Scalability:**
  I've introduced a dedicated section on performance optimization. This includes detailed strategies for profiling and benchmarking your workflows, enhancing the efficiency of both node execution and data handling across distributed systems.
- **Community-Driven Enhancements:**
  In response to feedback from our readers and the vibrant Flowise AI community, we've incorporated new insights, troubleshooting tips, and best practices shared by developers on the front lines of AI

innovation. These improvements ensure that the content not only reflects cutting-edge technology but also real-world challenges and solutions.

- **Future-Proofing Your Skills:**
  The new edition anticipates emerging trends in AI and lays out a roadmap for continued learning and adaptation. We've added forward-looking discussions on integrating AI with emerging fields such as edge computing and IoT, helping you stay ahead of the curve.

These improvements make the second edition a robust, comprehensive resource designed to empower you with the latest knowledge and practical tools to build, optimize, and scale AI workflows using Flowise AI.

C. Acknowledgments

I extend my heartfelt gratitude to everyone who has contributed to the creation and success of *Flowise AI: A Developer's Guide to Building LLM Applications, RAG Systems, and Agentic Workflows*. This second edition would not have been possible without the invaluable support, insights, and collaborative spirit of our community.

- **Community Contributors:**
  My deepest gratitude goes to the global network of developers, researchers, and enthusiasts who continuously share their knowledge and provide constructive feedback. Your contributions—from bug reports and feature suggestions to open-source code enhancements—have greatly enriched this work.
- **Beta Readers and Technical Reviewers:**
  Special thanks to the dedicated beta readers and technical experts who rigorously tested the concepts, code examples, and workflows presented in this book. Your thorough reviews and insightful critiques have helped ensure that the content is both accurate and accessible, bridging the gap between theory and real-world application.
- **Collaborators and Mentors:**
  We acknowledge the guidance and support of our mentors and industry peers, whose expertise in AI and software development has been instrumental in shaping the direction and depth of this edition. Your advice and encouragement have propelled us to explore new horizons and incorporate innovative solutions.
- **Family and Friends:**
  Heartfelt thanks to our families and friends for their unwavering

support and understanding. Your patience and belief in our vision have been the foundation upon which this book was built.

- **The Flowise AI Team:**
  Finally, we are grateful to the entire Flowise AI development team. Your passion for innovation and commitment to excellence have not only driven the evolution of Flowise AI but have also inspired us to continuously push the boundaries of what is possible in AI-driven workflows.

Thank you all for being part of this journey. Your collective efforts have made this second edition a testament to the power of community, collaboration, and relentless curiosity in the field of AI.

D. How to Use This Book

This book is designed to serve as both a comprehensive reference and a practical guide, tailored to meet the needs of developers ranging from beginners to seasoned professionals. Here are some tips on how to make the most out of this resource:

- **Start with the Foundations:**
  If you're new to Flowise AI or to building AI workflows in general, begin with the introductory chapters. The initial sections provide the necessary background, fundamental concepts, and step-by-step tutorials that will help you grasp the core principles before moving on to more advanced topics.
- **Follow the Roadmap:**
  The book is structured to gradually build your knowledge. Each chapter builds on the previous ones, so following the sequence can enhance your understanding. Use the detailed roadmap in Part I to plan your learning path.
- **Engage with Practical Examples:**
  Throughout the book, you'll find code snippets, walkthroughs, and real-world case studies. Actively work through these examples on your own system. Hands-on practice is key to mastering the techniques discussed.
- **Utilize Visual Aids:**
  Look for diagrams, flowcharts, and tables that break down complex concepts. These visual elements are designed to complement the text and provide clarity on workflow structures, system architectures, and process flows.

- **Customize Your Learning Experience:**
  Not every section will be relevant to every reader. Feel free to jump ahead to topics that align with your specific needs—whether that's advanced API integrations, agentic workflows, or deployment strategies. The comprehensive index and detailed table of contents will help you locate the sections most pertinent to your projects.
- **Reference the Appendices:**
  The appendices offer additional resources such as a glossary of key terms, an in-depth API reference, troubleshooting guides, and extra case studies. Use these sections to deepen your understanding and resolve any questions that arise as you work through the book.
- **Engage with the Community:**
  Beyond the book, join online forums, discussion groups, and Flowise AI community channels. Sharing experiences and solutions with other developers can provide valuable insights and enhance your learning journey.

By using this book as a flexible, interactive guide, you can not only learn the technical details of Flowise AI but also discover best practices, innovative techniques, and practical strategies that will help you build robust, scalable AI workflows. Enjoy your journey into the world of Flowise AI!

Part I: Foundations of Flowise AI

Chapter 1: Introduction to Flowise AI

1.1 Overview and Mission

Flowise AI is an innovative, open-source platform designed to simplify and accelerate the development of sophisticated AI workflows. At its core, Flowise AI empowers developers by providing a user-friendly visual interface alongside the flexibility of deep code-level customization. This dual approach makes it accessible to both newcomers in the AI space and seasoned professionals looking to build, optimize, and deploy advanced systems.

Overview

Flowise AI abstracts the complexity of integrating multiple AI components—such as large language models (LLMs), retrieval-augmented generation (RAG) systems, and agentic workflows—into a coherent, modular framework. Developers can visually design their workflows using a drag-and-drop interface that connects discrete nodes representing tasks like data input, processing, and output. This intuitive system enables rapid prototyping while maintaining the rigor required for production-level applications.

Key features include:

- **Modularity and Extensibility:** Each node is a self-contained component that can be configured, extended, or replaced, allowing developers to tailor workflows to specific project requirements.
- **Integration with Leading AI Frameworks:** Native support for modern LLMs and data retrieval systems ensures that the platform stays at the cutting edge of AI technology.
- **Scalable and Flexible Deployments:** Whether running locally or on the cloud, Flowise AI is built to scale—from simple experiments to enterprise-level applications.

Mission

The mission of Flowise AI is to democratize the development of advanced AI applications by:

- **Lowering the Barrier to Entry:** By providing an intuitive, visual approach to designing AI workflows, Flowise AI makes it easier for developers of all skill levels to harness the power of AI.
- **Accelerating Innovation:** Rapid prototyping, seamless integration of advanced AI components, and real-time feedback enable developers to iterate quickly and push the boundaries of what's possible.
- **Fostering Community Collaboration:** An active, open-source community drives continuous improvement, ensuring that Flowise AI evolves in response to real-world challenges and emerging trends.
- **Ensuring Scalability and Reliability:** By building a platform that supports both local and cloud deployments, Flowise AI helps organizations deploy robust, production-grade AI solutions that can adapt to growing demands.

This chapter sets the stage for exploring the many facets of Flowise AI. It lays out the foundational concepts and the guiding principles behind the platform, ensuring you have a clear understanding of both its capabilities and its strategic vision. As you progress through this book, you'll see how these core principles translate into practical, hands-on workflows and how Flowise AI can transform the way you build and deploy AI applications.

1.1.1 The Evolution of Flowise AI

Flowise AI has undergone a remarkable evolution since its inception, transforming from a simple workflow orchestration tool into a comprehensive, community-driven platform for advanced AI applications.

- **Early Beginnings:**
  Initially, Flowise AI was developed as a response to the growing need for a tool that could simplify the integration of emerging AI technologies. In its first iterations, it focused on basic workflow orchestration and provided developers with a straightforward visual interface to connect pre-built modules for data input, processing, and output.
- **Community-Driven Innovation:**
  As interest in AI grew, so did the contributions from a passionate global community. Open-source developers quickly began extending Flowise AI's capabilities, adding support for more sophisticated tasks such as natural language processing and real-time data retrieval. This collaborative spirit transformed Flowise AI into a dynamic platform where community contributions fueled rapid innovation.

- **Integration of Advanced AI Frameworks:**
  With the advent of large language models (LLMs) and retrieval-augmented generation (RAG) systems, Flowise AI evolved to include seamless integration with these state-of-the-art technologies. This milestone allowed the platform to move beyond basic workflow automation, enabling the development of applications that could generate, analyze, and transform human-like text, all while referencing real-time data.
- **Expansion into Agentic Workflows:**
  Recognizing the need for more autonomous and scalable systems, subsequent versions of Flowise AI introduced agentic workflows. This innovative approach broke down complex processes into independent, yet coordinated, agents that could execute tasks in parallel. The evolution into agentic workflows not only enhanced the platform's flexibility but also set a new standard for how AI-driven systems could be designed and managed.
- **Continuous Improvement and Future Readiness:**
  Today, Flowise AI stands as a mature, versatile platform that is continuously updated to incorporate the latest technological advancements and best practices. The evolution of Flowise AI reflects an ongoing commitment to making advanced AI accessible, reliable, and scalable—ensuring that developers can build cutting-edge solutions that meet the challenges of tomorrow.

This evolutionary journey illustrates Flowise AI's transformation from a simple workflow tool to a robust, all-encompassing platform that is at the forefront of AI innovation. The lessons learned and the community's collaborative efforts have shaped Flowise AI into a tool that not only meets current needs but is also poised to adapt to the rapidly changing landscape of artificial intelligence.

1.1.2 Community and Open-Source Impact

The growth and success of Flowise AI are deeply intertwined with the vibrant community and open-source contributions that have fueled its evolution. From the very beginning, community involvement has been at the heart of the platform, shaping its development, features, and real-world applicability.

- **Collaborative Development:**
  Open-source contributors from around the world have played a pivotal role in extending Flowise AI's capabilities. By sharing code,

proposing new features, and fixing bugs, these developers have helped transform the platform into a flexible and robust tool that meets the diverse needs of its users.

- **Innovation Through Feedback:**
  The community has consistently provided valuable insights through forums, discussion groups, and beta testing programs. This direct feedback loop has driven the rapid integration of cutting-edge AI technologies and best practices, ensuring that Flowise AI remains at the forefront of innovation.

- **Knowledge Sharing and Education:**
  Beyond code contributions, community members actively engage in creating tutorials, documentation, and case studies that demystify complex AI concepts. This collaborative learning environment not only accelerates skill development for new users but also cultivates a culture of continuous improvement and knowledge exchange.

- **Real-World Validation:**
  Numerous real-world projects and applications built by community members serve as a testament to Flowise AI's versatility and power. These projects provide concrete examples of how the platform can be adapted to solve a wide array of challenges—from intelligent chatbots and automated content generation to complex, multi-agent workflows in enterprise settings.

- **A Sustainable Ecosystem:**
  The open-source nature of Flowise AI fosters a sustainable ecosystem where innovation is both shared and built upon. The collective efforts of developers, researchers, and enthusiasts ensure that the platform evolves to address emerging trends and remains a relevant tool in the fast-paced world of AI.

In essence, the community and open-source contributions are not just an add-on to Flowise AI—they are integral to its DNA. They drive the platform's continuous improvement, ensuring that it stays adaptable, innovative, and capable of meeting the demands of modern AI applications.

1.2 Key Concepts

Flowise AI is built on several foundational pillars that empower developers to create robust, scalable, and intelligent AI workflows. In this section, we introduce the three core concepts that underpin the platform, each playing a crucial role in its versatility and effectiveness:

- **Large Language Models (LLMs):**
  These are deep neural networks trained on extensive corpora of text, enabling them to understand, generate, and manipulate human language. LLMs form the basis for various applications, such as chatbots, content generation, translation, and summarization. In Flowise AI, LLMs are integrated as nodes that can be easily configured to process and generate text, providing the natural language capabilities needed to drive intelligent workflows.
- **Retrieval-Augmented Generation (RAG) Systems:**
  RAG systems enhance the performance of LLMs by supplementing them with relevant external data. By retrieving context-specific documents or data points before generating a response, RAG systems improve the factual accuracy and relevance of the output. In Flowise AI, RAG is implemented as a combination of data retrieval nodes and generative LLM nodes, creating workflows that deliver enriched, context-aware responses for tasks like customer support, research, and knowledge management.
- **Agentic Workflows:**
  These workflows are characterized by their use of autonomous, modular agents that execute discrete tasks within a broader process. Each agent operates independently yet communicates with other agents to achieve a collective goal. Agentic workflows enable complex operations to be broken down into manageable, parallel processes, leading to enhanced scalability and fault tolerance. Flowise AI leverages this concept by allowing developers to design multi-agent systems where each agent can be customized, monitored, and optimized individually, ensuring efficient execution of even the most intricate workflows.

Understanding these key concepts is essential to fully grasp the capabilities of Flowise AI. As you progress through the chapters, you'll see how these elements come together to form a cohesive platform that simplifies the construction, deployment, and scaling of advanced AI applications.

1.2.1 Large Language Models (LLMs)

Large Language Models (LLMs) are at the core of modern AI applications, enabling machines to understand and generate human-like text with remarkable fluency and contextual awareness. These models are built on deep neural network architectures and trained on vast amounts of text data, which equips them with the ability to perform a wide range of language tasks.

Key Attributes of LLMs:

- **Scale and Complexity:**
  LLMs are trained on billions of words from diverse sources. This extensive training allows them to capture intricate patterns in language, leading to high-quality text generation and understanding.
- **Versatility:**
  They can be fine-tuned to perform various tasks such as translation, summarization, question answering, and content creation. This versatility makes them invaluable in multiple applications—from chatbots to advanced content generation.
- **Contextual Understanding:**
  LLMs excel at grasping context, enabling them to generate responses that are coherent and contextually relevant. This quality is essential for creating interactive, human-like dialogues in conversational AI systems.

LLMs in Flowise AI:

Within the Flowise AI platform, LLMs are seamlessly integrated as specialized nodes that empower developers to embed natural language processing capabilities directly into their workflows. Here's how they contribute to the platform:

- **Modular Integration:**
  Developers can easily incorporate LLMs into their workflows using dedicated nodes, which allow for straightforward configuration and customization of language tasks. Whether you're generating text, summarizing documents, or responding to user queries, the LLM nodes provide the foundational language capabilities.
- **Customization and Fine-Tuning:**
  Flowise AI supports the fine-tuning of LLMs for specific domains or tasks, ensuring that the generated outputs are tailored to meet the unique requirements of different applications. This customization helps in achieving more precise and relevant results.
- **Enhanced User Interactions:**
  By leveraging LLMs, Flowise AI facilitates the creation of intelligent chatbots and interactive applications that can engage users in natural, meaningful conversations. The contextual understanding provided by LLMs plays a pivotal role in generating responses that resonate with the user's intent.

In summary, Large Language Models represent a transformative advancement in artificial intelligence. Their ability to understand and generate human-like text, combined with their flexible integration within the Flowise AI ecosystem, makes them a cornerstone of modern AI workflows. As you explore further into this book, you will see practical examples of how LLMs are utilized to drive innovation and build sophisticated applications in various domains.

1.2.2 Retrieval-Augmented Generation (RAG) Systems

Retrieval-Augmented Generation (RAG) systems represent a significant advancement in the field of natural language processing. By combining the strengths of large language models with robust data retrieval techniques, RAG systems deliver responses that are not only contextually coherent but also factually enriched.

Key Attributes of RAG Systems:

- **Contextual Enrichment:**
  RAG systems first retrieve relevant documents or data from an external repository, then use that information as context to guide the generation of responses. This dual approach helps mitigate issues like hallucinations, ensuring that outputs are grounded in real, verifiable data.
- **Enhanced Accuracy:**
  By integrating up-to-date external knowledge with generative models, RAG systems produce more accurate and informed responses. This is especially critical in scenarios where factual correctness is paramount, such as customer support or information retrieval.
- **Dynamic Adaptability:**
  RAG systems are designed to adapt to new information. As external data sources are updated, the system can retrieve the most current information, thereby keeping responses relevant and timely.

RAG Systems in Flowise AI:

Within the Flowise AI platform, RAG systems are implemented as a synergy between data retrieval nodes and LLM nodes. This integration allows developers to build workflows that leverage both static pre-trained knowledge and dynamic, real-time data.

- **Seamless Integration:**
  Dedicated nodes in Flowise AI are configured to perform data retrieval tasks from document stores or APIs. The retrieved data is then fed into LLM nodes, which generate responses that are enhanced with this additional context.
- **Configurable Workflows:**
  Developers can tailor the retrieval process by specifying parameters such as data sources, query filters, and indexing strategies. This flexibility ensures that the RAG system can be optimized for various use cases, from generating detailed reports to answering specific queries.
- **Improved User Experience:**
  The combination of retrieval and generation results in richer, more informative outputs. Users benefit from responses that not only read naturally but also reflect current, relevant information drawn from comprehensive data repositories.

Retrieval-Augmented Generation systems are a powerful tool in the modern AI toolkit. By merging the generative capabilities of LLMs with the precision of data retrieval, RAG systems in Flowise AI enable the creation of workflows that are both intelligent and factually robust. As you delve deeper into this book, you will explore practical examples and case studies that illustrate how RAG systems can be implemented to build more accurate and context-aware AI applications.

1.2.3 Agentic Workflows

Agentic Workflows represent a transformative approach to building AI systems by breaking complex processes into independent, autonomous units known as agents. Each agent is designed to perform a specific task within a larger workflow, collaborating with other agents through well-defined communication channels. This modularity not only simplifies the design of complex systems but also enhances scalability, fault tolerance, and efficiency.

Key Attributes of Agentic Workflows:

- **Autonomy:**
  Each agent operates independently, making decisions based on predefined rules or dynamically adapting to real-time inputs. This autonomy allows agents to function without constant oversight, facilitating parallel processing.

- **Modularity:**
  By decomposing a workflow into discrete agents, developers can easily modify, replace, or upgrade individual components without overhauling the entire system. This modular design supports rapid iteration and experimentation.
- **Coordination and Communication:**
  Despite their independence, agents are designed to interact seamlessly. Well-defined communication protocols ensure that data and decisions flow smoothly between agents, creating a cohesive and coordinated operation across the entire workflow.
- **Scalability and Resilience:**
  Agentic workflows can scale horizontally by adding more agents to handle increased loads or more complex tasks. This structure also enhances fault tolerance; if one agent encounters an issue, it can be isolated and addressed without compromising the entire workflow.

Agentic Workflows in Flowise AI:

Within the Flowise AI platform, agentic workflows are implemented to manage and optimize complex, multi-step processes. Here's how they contribute to the platform's functionality:

- **Flexible Design:**
  Flowise AI allows developers to design workflows where each node or agent is responsible for a specific function—such as data input, processing, decision-making, or output generation. This setup mirrors real-world processes where tasks are distributed across specialized units.
- **Enhanced Efficiency:**
  By enabling agents to operate concurrently, Flowise AI can process large volumes of data or execute multiple tasks simultaneously. This parallelism leads to faster execution times and more efficient resource utilization.
- **Customizable Interactions:**
  Developers can define how agents interact, set communication protocols, and configure data exchange formats. This customization ensures that the workflow is perfectly aligned with the specific requirements of the application, whether it's for customer support, content generation, or data analysis.
- **Robust Error Handling:**
  The modular nature of agentic workflows means that if one agent fails, the system can isolate the issue, log the error, and continue

operating with minimal disruption. This resilience is critical in production environments where continuous operation is essential.

Agentic Workflows redefine how complex AI systems are designed and executed by leveraging the power of autonomous, modular agents. In Flowise AI, this approach provides a flexible, scalable, and resilient framework that empowers developers to build sophisticated workflows capable of handling intricate tasks with efficiency and precision. As you progress through this book, you'll encounter detailed examples and case studies illustrating how agentic workflows can be applied to solve real-world challenges, making your AI applications more robust and adaptive.

1.3 Flowise AI in the Modern AI Ecosystem

Flowise AI is designed to thrive within today's dynamic AI ecosystem, where rapid advancements and diverse technological integrations drive innovation. In this context, Flowise AI serves as a bridge between complex AI components and real-world applications, enabling developers to leverage state-of-the-art technologies with ease.

Positioning Within the Ecosystem:

- **Integration with Cutting-Edge Technologies:**
  Flowise AI seamlessly integrates with advanced Large Language Models (LLMs), Retrieval-Augmented Generation (RAG) systems, and agentic workflows. By doing so, it provides a unified platform that taps into the best of both generative and retrieval-based approaches. This integration ensures that applications built with Flowise AI can generate human-like text while also grounding outputs in real, verifiable data.
- **Interoperability and Flexibility:**
  Recognizing that no single tool can address every AI challenge, Flowise AI is built for interoperability. It easily connects with external APIs, document stores, and third-party services, allowing developers to customize their workflows and extend functionality. This modular architecture supports a wide range of applications— from intelligent chatbots to data-driven decision-making systems.
- **Scalability for Modern Demands:**
  Whether deployed locally or in cloud environments, Flowise AI is designed to scale. Its flexible deployment strategies, including support for containerization and orchestration tools like Docker and

Kubernetes, make it suitable for both small-scale experiments and enterprise-level solutions.

- **Community-Driven Evolution:**
  The ongoing contributions from a global community of developers and open-source enthusiasts ensure that Flowise AI remains current with emerging trends. This collective effort not only fuels continuous improvement but also ensures that the platform adapts to the evolving needs of the modern AI landscape.

Real-World Impact:

Flowise AI's integration into the modern AI ecosystem is exemplified by its real-world applications:

- **Intelligent Virtual Assistants:** Combining LLMs with real-time data retrieval to create conversational agents that are both responsive and factually accurate.
- **Automated Content Generation:** Enabling marketing teams and content creators to generate high-quality, context-aware text, reducing the time and effort required for content production.
- **Data Processing Pipelines:** Streamlining complex data workflows by orchestrating multiple autonomous agents, ensuring efficient, reliable processing across diverse data sources.

Flowise AI is more than just a tool—it's a comprehensive platform that encapsulates the latest advancements in AI technology. By positioning itself at the intersection of cutting-edge models, seamless integrations, and scalable architectures, Flowise AI empowers developers to build innovative solutions that meet the demands of today's AI-driven world. As you progress through this book, you will discover how Flowise AI leverages its unique capabilities to transform complex AI challenges into streamlined, actionable workflows.

1.3.1 Integration with Cutting-Edge Technologies

Flowise AI is designed to harness and integrate the latest breakthroughs in artificial intelligence, ensuring that developers have access to state-of-the-art tools and methodologies. By incorporating cutting-edge technologies, Flowise AI stays ahead of the curve, enabling you to build sophisticated and highly adaptive workflows. Here's how the platform achieves this integration:

- **Advanced Language Models:**
  Flowise AI seamlessly incorporates powerful Large Language Models (LLMs) that are constantly evolving. These models, such as OpenAI's GPT series and other leading architectures, provide robust natural language processing capabilities that power text generation, summarization, translation, and more. This integration allows you to embed high-quality language understanding directly into your workflows.

- **Retrieval-Augmented Generation (RAG):**
  To enhance the accuracy and relevance of AI-generated content, Flowise AI integrates RAG systems. This approach enriches generative outputs by retrieving pertinent data from external sources, ensuring that responses are not only contextually accurate but also fact-checked against up-to-date information. The synergy between retrieval and generation technologies enables more reliable and informative outputs.

- **Autonomous and Agentic Workflows:**
  The platform leverages the concept of agentic workflows, where independent agents perform specialized tasks. These agents work in tandem to handle complex processes, such as dynamic decision-making, parallel processing, and fault isolation. This modular and autonomous approach ensures that the system can adapt to changing conditions and scale efficiently, reflecting the latest innovations in distributed AI systems.

- **Cloud-Native and Containerized Environments:**
  Recognizing the importance of scalable deployment, Flowise AI integrates modern cloud-native technologies. Support for containerization with Docker and orchestration with Kubernetes ensures that workflows can be deployed reliably and scaled seamlessly across diverse environments. This integration supports real-time updates and continuous integration/continuous deployment (CI/CD) practices, making it easier to adopt and manage cutting-edge AI solutions in production.

- **Interoperability with External Services:**
  Flowise AI is built to be highly interoperable, allowing integration with various external APIs, data sources, and third-party services. Whether it's connecting to cloud-based databases, integrating with external monitoring tools, or leveraging specialized AI services, Flowise AI's flexible architecture makes it simple to incorporate and benefit from the latest technological advancements.

By embedding these cutting-edge technologies into its core, Flowise AI not only keeps pace with the rapid developments in the AI field but also provides a future-proof platform that empowers developers to innovate and solve complex challenges with confidence. As you explore the rest of this book, you'll discover how these integrations translate into real-world applications, enhancing both the functionality and scalability of your AI workflows.

1.3.2 Real-World Use Cases and Case Studies

Flowise AI's versatility is best demonstrated through its application in a wide range of real-world scenarios. By combining advanced language models, RAG systems, and agentic workflows, Flowise AI enables developers to build solutions that tackle complex challenges across various industries. Here are some key use cases and illustrative case studies:

- **Intelligent Virtual Assistants:**
  Flowise AI has been used to develop sophisticated chatbots and virtual assistants that understand user queries in natural language. By integrating LLMs with RAG systems, these assistants can provide context-aware responses that are both conversational and factually accurate.
  Case Study: A customer support chatbot for an e-commerce platform retrieves relevant policy documents in real time and generates detailed, personalized responses to help users navigate returns and exchanges.
- **Automated Content Generation:**
  Marketing teams and content creators leverage Flowise AI to generate articles, reports, and creative content. The platform's ability to fine-tune LLMs for specific writing styles, combined with real-time data retrieval, ensures that generated content is both engaging and up-to-date.
  Case Study: A media company deployed a workflow that automatically produces draft articles on emerging trends by aggregating the latest industry reports, which are then refined and human-edited for publication.
- **Data Processing and Analysis Pipelines:**
  In data-intensive environments, Flowise AI orchestrates multi-agent workflows to extract, process, and analyze large datasets. Agents can work in parallel to clean, transform, and summarize data, ultimately delivering actionable insights.
  Case Study: A financial services firm built a data processing pipeline that ingested quarterly reports, processed key financial metrics, and

generated executive summaries, significantly reducing manual analysis time.

- **Knowledge Management and Research Assistance:**
RAG systems powered by Flowise AI support knowledge management by dynamically retrieving and summarizing information from large document repositories. This is particularly useful in research and legal domains where accuracy and context are critical. *Case Study:* A law firm implemented an AI-driven research assistant that quickly pulls relevant case law and legal precedents, allowing attorneys to focus on analysis rather than extensive manual research.

- **Scalable Enterprise Automation:**
With its robust agentic workflow capabilities, Flowise AI enables the automation of complex enterprise processes, from customer onboarding to automated reporting. The platform's scalability ensures that these workflows can adapt to increasing loads and evolving business requirements.
Case Study: An insurance company utilized Flowise AI to streamline its claims processing workflow, deploying multiple autonomous agents to handle verification, data entry, and preliminary assessment, leading to faster processing times and improved customer satisfaction.

Each of these real-world applications not only highlights the technical capabilities of Flowise AI but also demonstrates how its flexible, integrated architecture can be tailored to solve diverse challenges. As you progress through this book, you will encounter detailed examples and hands-on projects that illustrate how these case studies have been implemented, providing you with a practical framework to build your own innovative AI solutions.

1.4 Roadmap and Learning Objectives

This chapter not only introduces you to the core concepts of Flowise AI but also sets the stage for your learning journey through this book. The roadmap and learning objectives outlined here are designed to help you navigate the content efficiently, ensuring that you build a solid foundation before moving on to more advanced topics. Below is an overview of what you can expect as you progress through the book and the key skills and insights you will gain:

Roadmap:

- **Foundational Concepts:**
  Begin with the fundamentals of Flowise AI, including its purpose, core components, and underlying technologies such as Large Language Models (LLMs), Retrieval-Augmented Generation (RAG) systems, and agentic workflows. This section will help you understand the building blocks and the rationale behind the platform.

- **Practical Setup and Initial Projects:**
  Move on to practical aspects by learning how to install Flowise AI, set up your environment, and create your first workflows. This part is designed to provide hands-on experience through guided tutorials and real-world examples, ensuring you're comfortable with the platform's interface and basic operations.

- **Deep Dive into Core Modules:**
  Explore the visual workflow builder in detail, including node customization and advanced integration with external APIs and services. You'll learn to configure, extend, and optimize workflows for various applications.

- **Advanced Applications:**
  Learn how to integrate cutting-edge AI technologies such as advanced LLMs, RAG systems, and multi-agent frameworks. This section includes in-depth case studies and practical projects that illustrate how to build complex, production-ready AI solutions.

- **Operational Excellence and Deployment:**
  Gain insights into deploying and managing AI workflows at scale, including topics such as cloud deployment, containerization with Docker and Kubernetes, CI/CD pipelines, and real-time monitoring and troubleshooting.

- **Future Directions:**
  Conclude with a look at emerging trends, best practices for continuous improvement, and strategies to keep your skills and projects future-proof as AI technologies continue to evolve.

Learning Objectives:

By the end of this book, you will be able to:

- **Understand and Articulate Core Concepts:**
  Explain the fundamental principles behind Flowise AI, including LLMs, RAG systems, and agentic workflows, and understand how they interact within the broader AI ecosystem.

- **Set Up and Configure Flowise AI:**
  Successfully install the platform, configure your development environment, and deploy Flowise AI both locally and in cloud-based environments.
- **Design and Build Workflows:**
  Create efficient, scalable workflows using the visual workflow builder, customize and extend nodes, and integrate external APIs and data sources to meet your specific project needs.
- **Leverage Advanced AI Integrations:**
  Implement advanced applications by integrating state-of-the-art LLMs and RAG systems, and design autonomous, multi-agent workflows that can process and analyze data in real time.
- **Optimize and Maintain AI Systems:**
  Apply best practices in performance tuning, error handling, and system monitoring to ensure that your AI applications run reliably and efficiently in production.
- **Plan for Future Innovations:**
  Stay informed about emerging trends in AI and understand how to adapt your workflows and development practices to incorporate new technologies and methodologies as they become available.

This roadmap and these objectives serve as your guide throughout the book. Whether you are new to AI development or an experienced practitioner, the structured progression is designed to equip you with both the theoretical understanding and the practical skills needed to master Flowise AI and build innovative, real-world applications.

Chapter 2: Getting Started with Flowise AI

2.1 System Requirements and Prerequisites

Before diving into Flowise AI, it's essential to ensure your system is properly equipped and all necessary prerequisites are in place. This section outlines the hardware, software, and additional dependencies required to get started smoothly.

Hardware Requirements

While Flowise AI is designed to be lightweight and scalable, performance can vary depending on the complexity of your workflows and the volume of data processed. Here are the recommended hardware specifications:

- **Processor:**
    - **Minimum:** Dual-core CPU
    - **Recommended:** Quad-core or higher for smoother multitasking and processing, especially when handling parallel agentic workflows.
- **Memory (RAM):**
    - **Minimum:** 4 GB
    - **Recommended:** 8 GB or more, particularly for running intensive LLM tasks or multiple workflows concurrently.
- **Disk Space:**
    - **Minimum:** 1 GB free space for installation and basic workflows
    - **Recommended:** 5 GB or more, especially if you plan to store extensive logs, run complex projects, or utilize local document stores.
- **Internet Connection:**
    - **Requirement:** A stable broadband connection is necessary for downloading dependencies, updates, and for cloud-based integrations.
    - **Recommended:** High-speed internet to ensure smooth operation during data retrieval and real-time API interactions.

Software Requirements

Flowise AI relies on several software components to function correctly. The following are the key software prerequisites:

- **Operating System:**
  - Compatible with modern operating systems such as:
    - Windows 10 or later
    - macOS 10.15 (Catalina) or later
    - Various Linux distributions (Ubuntu, Fedora, etc.)
- **Programming Languages and Runtime Environments:**
  - **Python:** Version 3.7 or later is required for executing code examples and running backend services.
  - **Node.js:** Some integration tools or front-end components may require Node.js. Ensure you have the latest stable version installed.
- **Containerization (Optional but Recommended):**
  - **Docker:** For simplified deployment and consistent environments across development and production, installing Docker is highly recommended. It allows you to encapsulate the entire Flowise AI environment into a portable container.
- **Version Control:**
  - **Git:** Essential for cloning the Flowise AI repository, tracking changes, and collaborating on workflows and custom node development.

Additional Prerequisites

- **Development Environment:**
  - **IDE or Code Editor:** Tools like VS Code, PyCharm, or Sublime Text can enhance your coding experience by providing features like syntax highlighting, debugging, and version control integration.
- **Dependencies and Libraries:**
  - Flowise AI comes with its own set of libraries and modules. During installation, these dependencies are typically managed via package managers (like pip for Python or npm for Node.js). Ensure you have access to the internet to download and update these packages.
- **System Configuration:**
  - **Firewall and Security Settings:** Ensure that your system's firewall settings allow for outgoing and incoming connections

on the ports used by Flowise AI (commonly port 3000 for the web interface). This is particularly important for cloud deployments or when integrating with external APIs.
- **Browser:**
  - o A modern web browser (Chrome, Firefox, Safari, or Edge) is required to access the Flowise AI dashboard. Ensure that your browser is up-to-date for the best compatibility and security.

Summary

Before proceeding with Flowise AI, verify that your system meets or exceeds these hardware and software requirements. Proper configuration and up-to-date dependencies not only ensure a smoother setup but also enhance performance and stability as you build and deploy your AI workflows.

With these prerequisites in place, you're ready to install Flowise AI and begin exploring its powerful features through hands-on tutorials and real-world projects.

2.1.1 Hardware and Software Considerations

Before installing Flowise AI, it's important to evaluate both your hardware and software environment to ensure optimal performance and compatibility. Here are the key factors to consider:

Hardware Considerations

- **Processor (CPU):**
  - o **Minimum Requirement:** A dual-core CPU is sufficient for basic workflows and small-scale projects.
  - o **Recommended:** A quad-core or higher processor is ideal, especially when running multiple processes concurrently or handling resource-intensive tasks like LLM operations and multi-agent workflows.
- **Memory (RAM):**
  - o **Minimum Requirement:** 4 GB of RAM to support basic operations and small projects.
  - o **Recommended:** 8 GB or more, particularly if you plan to run complex workflows, multiple nodes, or heavy data processing in parallel.
- **Storage:**

- o **Minimum Requirement:** At least 1 GB of free space for the Flowise AI installation and basic workflows.
  - o **Recommended:** 5 GB or more to accommodate large datasets, logs, and additional dependencies, especially when working with extensive document stores.
- **Internet Connectivity:**
  - o A stable and high-speed internet connection is critical for downloading dependencies, updates, and for integrating with external APIs and cloud services.

Software Considerations

- **Operating System:**
  - o Flowise AI is compatible with modern operating systems such as Windows 10 or later, macOS 10.15 (Catalina) or later, and popular Linux distributions (e.g., Ubuntu, Fedora).
- **Programming Environment:**
  - o **Python:** Ensure that you have Python 3.7 or later installed, as many components and code examples in Flowise AI are based on Python.
  - o **Node.js:** Some components, especially those related to the front-end interface or specific integrations, may require Node.js. Use the latest stable version for the best performance.
- **Containerization Tools:**
  - o **Docker (Optional but Recommended):** Docker provides a consistent runtime environment, simplifies the setup process, and facilitates scalable deployments across different systems.
- **Development Tools:**
  - o **IDE or Code Editor:** Tools like VS Code, PyCharm, or Sublime Text can enhance your productivity with features like syntax highlighting, debugging, and integrated version control.
  - o **Git:** Version control is essential for collaborating on projects, tracking changes, and managing custom node development within Flowise AI.

Summary

By ensuring that your hardware meets the recommended specifications and that you have the necessary software and development tools installed, you set a strong foundation for a smooth Flowise AI experience. Proper preparation in these areas not only enhances performance and stability but also paves the way for efficient development and deployment of advanced AI workflows.

2.1.2 Required Dependencies (Python, Node.js, Docker, etc.)

To get the most out of Flowise AI, you'll need to ensure that several key dependencies are installed and properly configured on your system. These dependencies provide the runtime environment, package management, and deployment flexibility needed to run and develop advanced AI workflows.

Python

- **Version Requirement:**
  Flowise AI requires Python 3.7 or later.
- **Purpose:**
  Python is used for executing backend services, running code examples, and managing AI libraries and modules.
- **Package Management:**
  Utilize pip (or pipenv/virtualenv) to manage and install the required Python packages specified in the project's requirements file.

Node.js

- **Version Requirement:**
  Ensure you have the latest stable version of Node.js installed.
- **Purpose:**
  Node.js is necessary for managing front-end components and certain integration tools within Flowise AI.
- **Package Management:**
  Use npm (or yarn) to install and update dependencies related to the web interface and related JavaScript libraries.

Docker (Optional but Recommended)

- **Purpose:**
  Docker provides a containerized environment that ensures consistency across development, testing, and production. It simplifies the deployment process and helps maintain the necessary environment configurations without manual setup.
- **Usage:**

o Pull the latest Flowise AI image using `docker pull flowiseai/flowise:latest`.
o Run containers using Docker commands to expose the interface on a desired port (e.g., port 3000).

Additional Dependencies and Tools

- **Git:**
  Essential for cloning the Flowise AI repository, version control, and collaborating on code changes.
- **Integrated Development Environment (IDE)/Code Editor:**
  Tools such as VS Code, PyCharm, or Sublime Text are recommended for enhanced coding experience through features like debugging, syntax highlighting, and integrated Git support.
- **Web Browser:**
  A modern web browser (Chrome, Firefox, Edge, or Safari) is required to access the Flowise AI dashboard. Make sure your browser is updated to the latest version for optimal performance and security.

Summary

Ensuring that you have Python 3.7 or later, the latest Node.js, and optionally Docker, along with Git and a suitable IDE, sets the stage for a smooth and productive experience with Flowise AI. These dependencies not only provide the backbone for development and execution but also enhance the portability and scalability of your AI workflows across different environments.

2.2 Installation and Setup

2.2.1 Local Installation and Docker Setup

Setting up Flowise AI locally is an excellent way to familiarize yourself with the platform and start building your own AI workflows. This section provides a step-by-step guide to installing Flowise AI on your local machine, including an option to use Docker for a containerized and reproducible environment.

Local Installation (Without Docker)

1. **Clone the Repository:**
   - o Open your terminal or command prompt.
   - o Clone the Flowise AI repository from GitHub:

   ```bash
   Copy code
   git clone
   https://github.com/flowiseai/flowise.git
   ```

   - o Navigate to the project directory:

   ```bash
   Copy code
   cd flowise
   ```

2. **Set Up a Python Virtual Environment (Optional but Recommended):**
   - o Create a virtual environment:

   ```nginx
   Copy code
   python3 -m venv venv
   ```

   - o Activate the virtual environment:
     - ▪ On macOS/Linux:

     ```bash
     Copy code
     source venv/bin/activate
     ```

     - ▪ On Windows:

     ```
     Copy code
     venv\Scripts\activate
     ```

3. **Install Python Dependencies:**
   - o Install the required Python packages using pip:

   ```nginx
   Copy code
   pip install -r requirements.txt
   ```

4. **Configure Environment Variables (If Necessary):**
    o Some components may require environment variables (e.g., API keys, configuration settings). Create a `.env` file in the project root and add the necessary variables as per the documentation.
5. **Run Flowise AI Locally:**
    o Start the application by running the main server file:

```
nginx
Copy code
python app.py
```

    o Open your web browser and navigate to `http://localhost:3000` (or the designated port) to access the Flowise AI dashboard.

Docker Setup

Docker provides a containerized environment that encapsulates all dependencies and configurations, ensuring consistency across different systems. Here's how to set up Flowise AI using Docker:

1. **Install Docker:**
    o If you haven't already, download and install Docker from Docker's official website.
2. **Pull the Latest Flowise AI Docker Image:**
    o Open your terminal and run:

```
bash
Copy code
docker pull flowiseai/flowise:latest
```

3. **Run the Docker Container:**
    o Launch a new container with the following command:

```
arduino
Copy code
docker run -d -p 3000:3000
flowiseai/flowise:latest
```

    o This command:

- Runs the container in detached mode (-d).
- Maps port 3000 of the container to port 3000 on your host machine (-p 3000:3000).

4. **Verify the Container is Running:**
   - Use the following command to check the running containers:

   ```nginx
   Copy code
   docker ps
   ```

   - You should see the Flowise AI container listed with the correct port mapping.

5. **Access Flowise AI:**
   - Open your web browser and navigate to http://localhost:3000 to view and interact with the Flowise AI dashboard.

Summary

Whether you choose to install Flowise AI directly on your system or utilize Docker for a containerized environment, both methods provide a reliable and efficient setup for developing AI workflows. Local installation gives you direct control over the environment, while Docker ensures consistency and ease of deployment across various platforms. Follow the steps above to get started, and once the installation is complete, you'll be ready to explore the powerful features of Flowise AI.

2.2.2 Cloud Deployment Options (AWS Marketplace, Azure, etc.)

Deploying Flowise AI in the cloud offers significant advantages in terms of scalability, reliability, and ease of maintenance. This section outlines several cloud deployment options, highlighting the benefits of each and providing guidance on how to set up Flowise AI on platforms such as AWS Marketplace, Azure, and other cloud services.

Key Benefits of Cloud Deployment

- **Scalability:**
  Cloud environments allow you to dynamically scale resources based on workload. This means that as your AI workflows grow in

complexity or demand, you can easily allocate more compute power or storage.

- **High Availability:**
Cloud providers offer robust infrastructure with built-in redundancy and failover mechanisms, ensuring that your applications remain accessible even in the event of hardware or network issues.
- **Managed Services:**
Many cloud platforms provide managed services for databases, container orchestration (e.g., Kubernetes), and continuous integration/continuous deployment (CI/CD) pipelines, reducing the operational overhead of managing the underlying infrastructure.
- **Global Reach:**
With data centers around the world, cloud deployment enables low-latency access for users regardless of their geographic location, making it easier to serve a global audience.

AWS Marketplace Deployment

- **Subscription Model:**
AWS Marketplace offers a simplified process to subscribe to and deploy Flowise AI. Once subscribed, you can launch pre-configured instances directly from the marketplace, with pricing models that suit your usage patterns.
- **Step-by-Step Deployment:**
  1. **Access the AWS Marketplace:** Navigate to the Flowise AI product page on AWS Marketplace.
  2. **Subscribe to the Product:** Review the subscription details, pricing, and terms of use. Click "Subscribe" to proceed.
  3. **Configuration:** Follow the prompts to configure your instance settings, including instance type (e.g., t3.medium or higher), region, and network settings (VPC, security groups, etc.).
  4. **Launch the Instance:** Once configured, launch your instance. AWS will provision the resources, and you will receive a public IP or domain name to access your Flowise AI dashboard.
  5. **Post-Deployment:** Use AWS tools for monitoring and managing the instance, ensuring optimal performance and uptime.

Azure Deployment Options

- **Azure Marketplace and Virtual Machines:**
  Similar to AWS, Microsoft Azure offers deployment through its
  Marketplace where you can find pre-configured images of Flowise
  AI. Alternatively, you can deploy Flowise AI on an Azure Virtual
  Machine for more granular control over the environment.
- **Containerized Deployments:**
  Azure Kubernetes Service (AKS) can be used to deploy Flowise AI
  in a containerized format. This approach leverages Docker containers
  orchestrated by Kubernetes, ensuring scalable, resilient, and easy-to-
  manage deployments.
- **Step-by-Step Guidance:**
  1. **Access Azure Marketplace:** Search for Flowise AI or related
     container images in the Azure Marketplace.
  2. **Select Deployment Model:** Choose between a managed
     service or deploying on a Virtual Machine/AKS, based on
     your requirements.
  3. **Configuration:** Set up instance size, storage options, and
     networking configurations.
  4. **Deployment and Monitoring:** Deploy your instance and
     utilize Azure's monitoring tools (e.g., Azure Monitor, Log
     Analytics) to track performance and troubleshoot issues.

Other Cloud Providers and Multi-Cloud Strategies

- **Google Cloud Platform (GCP):**
  GCP offers similar services with its Compute Engine, Kubernetes
  Engine, and Marketplace solutions. You can deploy Flowise AI using
  containerized applications on GCP for flexibility and scalability.
- **Multi-Cloud Deployments:**
  For enterprises looking to minimize vendor lock-in or optimize for
  different geographic regions, a multi-cloud strategy might be ideal.
  This involves deploying Flowise AI across multiple cloud platforms,
  ensuring high availability and resilience through redundancy.

Summary

Cloud deployment of Flowise AI provides a flexible, scalable, and highly
available solution for managing complex AI workflows. Whether you choose
AWS Marketplace, Azure, GCP, or a multi-cloud approach, leveraging the

strengths of these platforms can help you maximize performance and efficiency. By following the deployment steps outlined above, you can ensure that your Flowise AI instance is well-configured, secure, and optimized for your specific use case.

2.3 Navigating the Flowise AI Interface

The Flowise AI interface is designed with both simplicity and power in mind, offering an intuitive, visually driven environment to build, manage, and monitor your AI workflows. This section provides a comprehensive guide to navigating the main components of the interface and understanding their roles.

Key Components of the Interface

- **Dashboard:**
  The dashboard serves as your command center. Here, you can:
  - View and manage your existing workflows.
  - Access recent projects and monitor system status.
  - Get quick insights into performance metrics and active processes.
- **Visual Workflow Builder:**
  The heart of Flowise AI, the visual workflow builder, allows you to:
  - Drag and drop nodes onto a canvas to create or modify workflows.
  - Arrange and connect nodes representing tasks (e.g., data input, processing, output) in a clear, visual manner.
  - See real-time representations of how data flows between nodes, making it easier to understand and debug your processes.
- **Node Library:**
  Typically located on the side panel, the Node Library contains:
  - A collection of pre-built nodes that perform specific functions.
  - Options to drag these nodes into your workflow canvas.
  - Access to custom or extended nodes, allowing you to tailor the workflow to your needs.
- **Properties Panel:**
  When you select a node on the canvas, the properties panel displays:
  - Detailed configuration settings for the node.

- Editable fields for parameters such as data sources, transformation options, and API configurations.
- Help text or tooltips that guide you in making the right adjustments for optimal performance.
- **Console/Logs Area:**
Located typically at the bottom or in a dedicated section:
  - Displays system messages, error logs, and output from node executions.
  - Helps in monitoring real-time activity and diagnosing issues within your workflow.
  - Provides feedback when workflows run, allowing you to verify that processes are executing as expected.

Navigational Tips

- **Getting Oriented:**
Start by exploring the dashboard to familiarize yourself with where your projects, workflows, and system statistics are located. Take a few minutes to click through the various sections before diving into workflow design.
- **Creating and Editing Workflows:**
  - Use the visual workflow builder to create a new workflow by dragging nodes from the Node Library onto the canvas.
  - Connect nodes by clicking on an output connector and dragging a link to the corresponding input connector of another node.
  - Double-click or select a node to open its properties in the Properties Panel, where you can adjust settings and parameters.
- **Using the Console for Troubleshooting:**
  - Monitor the console/logs area to watch how data flows through your workflow in real time.
  - Use error messages and logs to pinpoint issues and adjust your workflow accordingly.
- **Customization and Experimentation:**
  - Don't hesitate to experiment with different node configurations or rearrangements on the canvas.
  - Save multiple versions of your workflows to compare performance and identify the best structure for your project.

Summary

Navigating the Flowise AI interface is all about leveraging its visual and interactive features to streamline your workflow design process. By understanding the dashboard, visual workflow builder, node library, properties panel, and console/logs area, you can effectively manage, troubleshoot, and optimize your AI projects. With practice, the interface becomes an invaluable tool in your development process, enabling you to focus on building robust and scalable AI workflows.

2.3.1 Dashboard Overview and Visual Workflow Builder

The Dashboard and Visual Workflow Builder form the core of the Flowise AI interface, offering a unified and intuitive environment for managing your AI projects and designing workflows.

Dashboard Overview

- **Central Command Center:**
  The Dashboard is your first stop upon logging in. It provides a comprehensive overview of your current projects, workflows, and system status. Here, you can:
  - **Access Projects:** Quickly view, open, or manage existing workflows and projects.
  - **Monitor Performance:** Check key metrics and real-time status updates to ensure your workflows are running smoothly.
  - **Quick Navigation:** Use the dashboard's intuitive layout to jump directly into the workflow builder or access support resources.
- **Activity Feed and Notifications:**
  Stay updated with the latest activity—whether it's recent changes to workflows, system alerts, or performance notifications. This feed helps you track progress and promptly address any issues.

Visual Workflow Builder

- **Interactive Canvas:**
  The Visual Workflow Builder is a drag-and-drop interface that allows you to visually design and modify your workflows. Key features include:

- o **Node Placement:** Easily drag nodes representing different tasks (data input, processing, output, etc.) onto the canvas.
- o **Connector Visualization:** Create connections between nodes to establish the flow of data. This visual representation helps you understand how information moves through the system.
- o **Real-Time Editing:** Make on-the-fly adjustments to your workflow. The builder supports dynamic changes, allowing you to tweak node configurations or re-arrange components as needed.
- **Intuitive Design Tools:**
  The builder includes helpful tools such as:
  - o **Zoom and Pan:** Navigate large or complex workflows with ease.
  - o **Alignment and Grid Layouts:** Ensure that your nodes are neatly arranged, making the workflow easier to read and manage.
  - o **Preview Mode:** Test and simulate workflow execution directly from the builder to verify logic and performance.
- **Seamless Integration with Other Interface Components:**
  - o **Properties Panel:** When you select a node in the builder, detailed configuration options appear in the Properties Panel, allowing you to customize each node's behavior.
  - o **Instant Feedback:** Errors, warnings, or execution logs are fed back in real time via the console, making it straightforward to identify and resolve issues.

Summary

The Dashboard and Visual Workflow Builder are designed to work together to provide a smooth and efficient development experience. The Dashboard gives you a bird's-eye view of your projects and system health, while the Visual Workflow Builder offers a hands-on, intuitive space to craft, adjust, and optimize your AI workflows. This integrated approach empowers you to rapidly prototype and iterate on solutions, ensuring that your development process remains both efficient and user-friendly.

2.3.2 Node Library, Properties Panel, and Log Monitoring

Flowise AI's interface is designed to provide you with powerful tools to create, customize, and monitor your AI workflows. This section dives into three key components: the Node Library, the Properties Panel, and the Log Monitoring area.

Node Library

- **Central Repository of Components:**
  The Node Library is a curated collection of pre-built nodes, each representing a specific function within your workflow—such as data input, processing, or output. These nodes serve as the building blocks for your workflows.
- **Ease of Use:**
  You can simply drag and drop nodes from the library onto the Visual Workflow Builder canvas. This intuitive approach allows you to quickly assemble complex workflows without having to write extensive code from scratch.
- **Customization Options:**
  In addition to standard nodes, the library may also include custom or extended nodes developed by the community or tailored to your specific needs. This ensures that you have the flexibility to adapt the platform to a wide range of applications.

Properties Panel

- **Dynamic Configuration:**
  When you select any node on the canvas, its configuration settings are displayed in the Properties Panel. This area allows you to fine-tune the behavior and parameters of each node.
- **User-Friendly Controls:**
  The panel provides various input fields, dropdowns, and toggles that enable you to adjust settings such as data sources, API keys, processing parameters, and more. Tooltips and help text often accompany these settings, making it easier for you to understand their function.
- **Real-Time Updates:**
  As you modify node settings, changes are immediately reflected in the workflow. This instant feedback loop helps ensure that your configurations are correct before running the workflow.

Log Monitoring

- **Real-Time Feedback:**
  The Log Monitoring area (often integrated with the Console) displays system messages, execution logs, and error reports in real time. This

functionality is crucial for debugging and optimizing your workflows.

- **Detailed Insights:**
  Logs provide detailed information about the operation of each node, including successful execution messages and warnings or errors if something goes wrong. This helps you quickly identify and resolve issues within your workflow.
- **Historical Context:**
  In addition to real-time monitoring, the log system often retains historical data, allowing you to review past executions. This can be invaluable for performance tuning and understanding the behavior of your workflows over time.

Summary

Together, the Node Library, Properties Panel, and Log Monitoring components create an integrated environment that empowers you to build, customize, and fine-tune your AI workflows efficiently. The Node Library provides the essential components, the Properties Panel offers dynamic configuration options, and the Log Monitoring area ensures you have the visibility needed to troubleshoot and optimize your system. This comprehensive suite of tools is designed to streamline your development process and enhance your overall experience with Flowise AI.

2.4 Building Your First Workflow: A Hands-On Tutorial

In this section, you'll create your very first workflow in Flowise AI. This hands-on tutorial will guide you through each step—from launching the interface to executing a simple workflow that processes and displays data. Follow along to gain practical experience with the platform.

Step 1: Launch the Flowise AI Interface

- **Access the Dashboard:**
  Open your web browser and navigate to your Flowise AI instance (e.g., `http://localhost:3000`). You'll be greeted by the Dashboard, which provides an overview of your projects and system status.
- **Log In (if required):**
  Enter your credentials to access the full suite of features available in the interface.

Step 2: Create a New Workflow

- **Start a New Project:**
  On the Dashboard, click the "New Workflow" button. A prompt will appear asking for a name—enter a descriptive name such as "FirstFlow."
- **Enter the Workflow Builder:**
  Once created, you will be taken to the Visual Workflow Builder, where you can design your workflow.

Step 3: Add Nodes to Your Workflow

- **Drag-and-Drop Nodes:**
  On the left side, locate the Node Library. For this tutorial, you will need three basic nodes:
  - **Data Input Node:** Simulates data collection.
  - **Processing Node:** Applies a simple transformation (e.g., converting text to uppercase).
  - **Output Node:** Displays the final result.
- **Place Nodes on the Canvas:**
  Drag each node from the Node Library onto the canvas, and position them in a logical sequence: first the Input, then Processing, and finally the Output.

Step 4: Connect the Nodes

- **Establish Data Flow:**
  - Click the output connector on the Data Input Node and drag a connection to the input connector of the Processing Node.
  - Similarly, connect the Processing Node to the Output Node.
- **Visual Verification:**
  The connections should be visible as lines between the nodes, indicating the flow of data from one stage to the next.

Step 5: Configure Each Node

- **Data Input Node Configuration:**
  - Select the Data Input Node to open the Properties Panel.
  - Configure it to output a simple text string, for example:
    `"Hello, Flowise AI!"`
- **Processing Node Configuration:**

- Select the Processing Node and configure it with a basic transformation function.
- For example, set the transformation to convert the input text to uppercase.
- If available, use a built-in option or add a small code snippet:

```python
Copy code
def to_uppercase(text):
    return text.upper()
```

- Assign this function in the node settings.
- **Output Node Configuration:**
  - Select the Output Node and ensure it is set up to display the processed result.
  - You might choose a simple display or logging option that prints the output to the screen.

Step 6: Execute the Workflow

- **Run the Workflow:**
  Click the "Run" button, typically located at the top of the interface.
- **Monitor Execution:**
  Check the Console/Log Monitoring area to view real-time updates. You should see a log indicating that the workflow started, processed the data, and generated an output.
- **Verify the Result:**
  The Output Node should display the transformed text. If the initial string was "Hello, Flowise AI!", you should now see it as "HELLO, FLOWISE AI!".

Step 7: Troubleshoot and Iterate

- **Review Logs:**
  If you encounter errors or unexpected behavior, review the logs in the Console for detailed error messages.
- **Adjust Node Settings:**
  Use the Properties Panel to fine-tune node configurations. For example, if the text isn't transforming as expected, double-check the processing function or parameters.

- **Re-run the Workflow:**
  After making any adjustments, re-run the workflow to verify that the changes yield the desired outcome.

Summary

By following this tutorial, you've built a simple yet complete workflow in Flowise AI:

- The **Data Input Node** collects the input text.
- The **Processing Node** applies a transformation (converting text to uppercase).
- The **Output Node** displays the final result.

This hands-on experience not only familiarizes you with the Flowise AI interface but also lays the groundwork for creating more complex workflows. As you progress, you can add additional nodes, experiment with advanced configurations, and integrate external data sources to further expand your AI applications.

Part II: Building Blocks and Core Modules

Chapter 3: The Visual Workflow Builder

3.1 Understanding Nodes, Connectors, and Data Flow

The Visual Workflow Builder in Flowise AI is a powerful tool that transforms complex programming logic into an intuitive, visual design process. At the heart of this builder are three fundamental elements: nodes, connectors, and the data flow. Each plays a crucial role in how your AI workflows are constructed, executed, and managed.

Nodes

- **Definition and Purpose:**
  Nodes are the fundamental building blocks of a workflow. Each node represents a discrete operation or function within your AI pipeline. They encapsulate specific tasks—such as gathering data, processing information, or generating output—making them modular and reusable components.
- **Types of Nodes:**
  - **Input Nodes:** Designed to collect or receive data from various sources, including files, databases, or external APIs.
  - **Processing Nodes:** Responsible for manipulating or analyzing the data. This might include operations like data transformation, filtering, or executing a custom code function.
  - **Output Nodes:** These nodes take the processed data and deliver it in a usable form, whether that's displaying results, writing to a file, or triggering subsequent actions.
- **Customization:**
  Each node can be configured via the Properties Panel to meet specific needs. Whether using built-in settings or integrating custom code, nodes can be tailored to perform precise tasks within your workflow.

Connectors

- **Definition and Purpose:**
  Connectors are the visual links that join nodes together. They define the path through which data flows from one node to another, ensuring that the output of one operation becomes the input for the next.

- **Directional Data Flow:**
  The connectors illustrate a clear, directional flow of data. This visualization helps you understand how data is being passed and transformed throughout the workflow, making it easier to troubleshoot and optimize processes.
- **Visual Feedback:**
  The presence of connectors not only maps out the logical sequence of operations but also provides immediate visual feedback on the structure and integrity of your workflow. If a connector is missing or misconfigured, it is often immediately apparent on the canvas.

Data Flow

- **Concept:**
  Data flow is the sequential movement of data through the nodes in your workflow. It represents the operational logic—how raw data enters the system, gets processed step by step, and finally produces an output.
- **Process Explanation:**
    - **Initiation:** Data is introduced into the workflow via an input node.
    - **Transformation:** The data is then processed by one or more processing nodes. Each processing step might perform functions like aggregation, filtering, or transformation, refining the data progressively.
    - **Final Output:** Ultimately, the transformed data is sent to an output node, where it is either displayed, stored, or passed on to another system.
- **Debugging and Optimization:**
  A well-designed data flow is crucial for ensuring that the workflow operates as intended. With real-time log monitoring and clear visualization provided by connectors, you can quickly identify where data might be misrouted, delayed, or improperly processed. This makes it easier to optimize and refine the workflow for efficiency and accuracy.

Summary

Understanding nodes, connectors, and data flow is essential for mastering the Visual Workflow Builder in Flowise AI. Nodes serve as the individual functional units that execute specific tasks, connectors create the necessary pathways for data to travel between these units, and the overall data flow defines the logical progression of operations from start to finish. With these concepts in hand, you can design robust, scalable, and easily maintainable AI workflows that effectively tackle complex tasks while providing clear visual feedback at every step.

3.1.1 Types of Nodes: Input, Processing, Output

Nodes are the essential elements that make up your workflows in Flowise AI. Each type of node plays a specific role, allowing you to break down complex processes into manageable, discrete operations. The three primary categories of nodes are Input, Processing, and Output, each contributing to the overall functionality of the workflow.

Input Nodes

- **Purpose:**
  Input nodes are designed to ingest data from various sources. They act as the entry point for your workflow, supplying the raw data that will be subsequently processed.
- **Common Functions:**
  - **Data Collection:** Fetch data from files, databases, APIs, or user inputs.
  - **Initial Formatting:** Perform preliminary transformations like parsing or data validation before passing the data along.
- **Example Use Case:**
  An input node might be configured to read a JSON file containing customer details, which then becomes the foundation for a subsequent data analysis workflow.

Processing Nodes

- **Purpose:**
  Processing nodes handle the transformation and manipulation of data. They are the workhorses of your workflow, where the core logic is applied to convert raw input into meaningful, actionable output.
- **Common Functions:**
  - **Data Transformation:** Modify or reformat data (e.g., converting text to uppercase, filtering out irrelevant information).
  - **Computation and Analysis:** Execute mathematical operations, statistical analysis, or apply machine learning models.

- o **Custom Logic:** Incorporate custom code snippets to perform specialized operations tailored to your application needs.
- **Example Use Case:**
  A processing node may take customer data from an input node and clean it by removing duplicates, normalizing text fields, or calculating aggregated metrics like total purchase amounts.

Output Nodes

- **Purpose:**
  Output nodes are responsible for delivering the final results of the workflow. They take the processed data and present it in a format that is useful for the end user or for subsequent systems.
- **Common Functions:**
  - o **Display Results:** Show the processed data on a dashboard or web interface.
  - o **Data Storage:** Save the output to a file, database, or send it via an API to another service.
  - o **Trigger Actions:** Initiate follow-up actions or alerts based on the output, such as sending notifications.
- **Example Use Case:**
  An output node might display a formatted report of customer insights on a dashboard, or store the analysis results in a cloud-based database for future reference.

Summary

In summary, the Input, Processing, and Output nodes work together to form a cohesive workflow. Input nodes bring data into the system, processing nodes transform and analyze that data, and output nodes ensure the results are effectively communicated or stored. By understanding and leveraging these different types of nodes, you can design and implement robust, scalable AI workflows that address a wide array of real-world applications.

3.1.2 Managing Data Flow and Debugging Workflows

A well-designed data flow is the backbone of any effective AI workflow. In Flowise AI, managing data flow involves overseeing how data is passed through various nodes, ensuring that each transformation or operation produces the expected results. Equally important is the ability to debug workflows—identifying and resolving issues quickly to maintain smooth operation. This section provides strategies and techniques to effectively manage data flow and debug your workflows.

Managing Data Flow

- **Defining Clear Data Pathways:**
  - Ensure that every node's output is correctly connected to the appropriate input node.
  - Use connectors to visually map out the sequential data movement from input to processing to output.
  - Maintain consistency in data formats and structures throughout the workflow to avoid mismatches or processing errors.
- **Monitoring Data Transformation:**
  - Regularly review intermediate data outputs to verify that transformations are occurring as expected.
  - Use test inputs and controlled data samples to simulate workflow execution and observe how data changes at each stage.
- **Implementing Checkpoints:**
  - Introduce validation nodes or checkpoints that inspect data at critical junctures.
  - These checkpoints can trigger alerts if the data deviates from expected patterns, helping catch issues early in the process.
- **Documenting Data Flow:**
  - Maintain clear documentation of the expected data schema at each stage of the workflow.
  - Annotate your connectors and nodes with brief descriptions of the data transformations, which aids both in debugging and future modifications.

Debugging Workflows

- **Real-Time Log Monitoring:**
  - Use the integrated log monitoring system to view real-time outputs and error messages from nodes.
  - The logs provide immediate feedback on workflow execution, enabling you to pinpoint where an error might be occurring.
- **Isolating Problematic Nodes:**
  - If an error occurs, try running individual nodes or smaller sub-sections of your workflow independently.

- o Isolating nodes helps identify whether the issue lies in the data input, the processing logic, or the output configuration.
- **Utilizing Breakpoints and Simulated Inputs:**
  - o Many workflows can be tested using simulated inputs. Use this feature to run a "dry test" that mimics real execution without affecting production data.
  - o Setting breakpoints or pauses between nodes allows you to inspect intermediate outputs and verify that data transformations are correct.
- **Iterative Refinement:**
  - o Debugging is often an iterative process. Make small, incremental changes to your node configurations and re-run the workflow to observe the impact.
  - o Document each change and its effect on the data flow, so that you can trace back the root cause of an issue.
- **Collaborative Debugging:**
  - o Engage with your team or community forums if you encounter persistent issues.
  - o Sharing log outputs and node configurations can help others provide insights and solutions based on similar experiences.

Summary

Managing data flow and debugging workflows are critical skills for ensuring that your AI applications run efficiently and accurately. By establishing clear data pathways, monitoring intermediate outputs, and utilizing real-time log monitoring, you can maintain robust workflows in Flowise AI. Combined with systematic debugging techniques—such as isolating nodes, using simulated inputs, and iteratively refining configurations—you'll be well-equipped to identify and resolve issues quickly, ensuring that your workflows are both resilient and optimized for performance.

3.2 Customizing and Extending Nodes

Flowise AI is designed to be flexible and adaptable, allowing you to tailor individual nodes to meet the specific needs of your workflows. Customizing and extending nodes not only enhances functionality but also enables you to integrate unique business logic or external services into your AI applications. This section covers how you can modify built-in node settings and extend their capabilities through custom code or entirely new node creations.

Customizing Built-In Nodes

- **Properties Panel Configuration:**
  Each built-in node comes with a set of configurable parameters accessible via the Properties Panel. Here, you can adjust settings such as data formats, transformation rules, or API endpoints without modifying underlying code. For example:
    - Change input types or validation rules for an Input Node.
    - Adjust processing options like text transformation methods in a Processing Node.
    - Configure output settings to determine how and where results are displayed or stored.
- **Parameter Tuning:**
  Fine-tune nodes by leveraging available options such as toggles, dropdown menus, or text fields. This allows you to quickly iterate on different configurations to optimize workflow performance.

Extending Node Functionality with Custom Code

- **Injecting Custom Logic:**
  When built-in configurations are insufficient, you can extend a node's behavior by injecting custom code. This can be accomplished in several ways:
    - **Custom Functions:** Write a function to perform a specific transformation or operation. For example, a custom processing function could reverse a string, perform complex data filtering, or integrate with an external API.
    - **Code Snippets in Nodes:** Some nodes allow you to insert code snippets directly in their configuration. This enables dynamic behavior without needing to modify the core system.
- **Example – Custom Processing Function:**
  Suppose you want a node that converts text to title case instead of the default uppercase. You might write:

```python
Copy code
def to_title_case(text):
    return text.title()
```

You would then assign this function to the Processing Node through its configuration settings. The node will now process incoming data using your custom function.

Creating New Nodes

- **Developing Custom Node Classes:**
  If your requirements extend beyond modifying existing nodes, you can create entirely new nodes. This involves:
  - **Defining a New Class:** Inherit from Flowise AI's base node class and implement required methods such as data processing, error handling, and configuration management.
  - **Implementing Core Methods:** Ensure your custom node supports essential functions like initialization, execution, and logging. This allows it to integrate seamlessly with the rest of the workflow builder.
- **Integration and Registration:**
  Once your custom node is developed, register it with the Flowise AI system so it appears in your Node Library. This step may involve updating configuration files or using dedicated commands provided by Flowise AI.
- **Example – Creating a Sentiment Analysis Node:**
  For instance, you could build a custom node that performs sentiment analysis on text inputs:

```python
Copy code
from flowise.nodes import BaseNode

class SentimentAnalysisNode(BaseNode):
    def __init__(self, name="SentimentAnalysisNode"):
        super().__init__(name)

    def process(self, input_data):
        # Integrate with a sentiment analysis API or
library
        sentiment = self.analyze_sentiment(input_data)
        return {"sentiment": sentiment, "input":
input_data}

    def analyze_sentiment(self, text):
        # For demonstration, return a mock sentiment
result
        return "positive" if "good" in text.lower()
else "neutral"
```

After defining the node, you register it so it becomes available for use in your workflows.

Best Practices for Customization

- **Maintain Readability and Modularity:**
  When writing custom code, keep it modular and well-documented. This makes it easier to debug, extend, and collaborate on your workflows.
- **Test Incrementally:**
  Test custom functions or nodes individually before integrating them into larger workflows. This iterative approach ensures that each component works as intended.
- **Leverage Community Resources:**
  Utilize documentation, forums, and community examples to guide your customization efforts. Many developers share their custom nodes and extensions, which can serve as valuable references.

Summary

Customizing and extending nodes in Flowise AI unlocks a higher level of flexibility and functionality within your workflows. By adjusting built-in configurations, injecting custom code, and developing entirely new node classes, you can tailor the platform to meet diverse application needs. This adaptability not only enhances your workflows but also fosters innovation by allowing you to integrate specialized logic and external services seamlessly. As you progress through this book, you'll discover additional techniques and examples that illustrate the power of customization in building advanced AI solutions.

3.2.1 Configuring Built-In Nodes

Built-in nodes in Flowise AI come pre-configured with a wide range of settings designed to cover common use cases. However, fine-tuning these nodes to suit your specific application requirements is key to building effective workflows. This section explains how to configure built-in nodes using the Properties Panel and other available tools.

Accessing Configuration Settings

- **Properties Panel:**
  When you select a node in the Visual Workflow Builder, its configuration options automatically appear in the Properties Panel.

This panel displays all relevant settings such as input parameters, processing options, and output formats.

- **Tooltips and Documentation:**
  Each configurable parameter is often accompanied by tooltips or help text. These descriptions explain what the parameter does and suggest typical values, providing guidance for both beginners and experienced users.

Key Configuration Options

- **Data Input and Validation:**
  For input nodes, you can define the expected data type (e.g., text, JSON, numeric), set default values, and implement validation rules to ensure the data conforms to expected formats. This helps prevent errors downstream in the workflow.
- **Processing Parameters:**
  Processing nodes typically offer a variety of parameters that dictate how data is transformed. These might include:
  - **Transformation Functions:** Choose from built-in functions (e.g., converting text to uppercase or lowercase) or insert custom functions.
  - **Thresholds and Filters:** Set numeric thresholds or filtering criteria to refine the data that is passed along.
  - **Custom Code Blocks:** Some nodes allow you to input small code snippets directly into the configuration, offering flexibility to implement bespoke processing logic without creating an entirely new node.
- **Output Settings:**
  Output nodes can be configured to determine the format and destination of the results. For instance:
  - **Display Options:** Choose whether to output data to a console, a dashboard element, or store it in a database.
  - **Formatting:** Set parameters for text formatting, report structure, or data serialization.

Parameter Tuning and Testing

- **Iterative Adjustment:**
  Start with default settings and then gradually adjust parameters based on the performance of your workflow. Use small increments in parameter changes to observe their impact on output and data flow.

- **Use of Simulated Inputs:**
  Before integrating nodes into a full workflow, test them with simulated or controlled input data. This allows you to validate the configuration and ensure that the node behaves as expected under various scenarios.
- **Real-Time Feedback:**
  Monitor logs and output data as you adjust configurations. The immediate feedback from the Console helps in verifying that changes are effective and in identifying any issues early in the setup process.

Best Practices for Configuration

- **Document Your Settings:**
  Maintain clear documentation or inline comments for custom configurations. This practice not only aids in future troubleshooting but also makes it easier for others to understand your workflow.
- **Keep It Modular:**
  Avoid overcomplicating node settings. If a node becomes too complex, consider breaking the functionality into smaller, dedicated nodes. This modular approach simplifies debugging and improves overall workflow clarity.
- **Leverage Community Examples:**
  Explore examples and case studies from the Flowise AI community. Many users share their configuration settings and customizations, which can serve as valuable references for optimizing your own workflows.

Summary

Configuring built-in nodes effectively is essential for tailoring Flowise AI to your project's needs. By using the Properties Panel, adjusting key parameters, and testing with simulated inputs, you can fine-tune nodes to ensure that they process data correctly and efficiently. This careful configuration lays a solid foundation for building robust, scalable AI workflows, allowing you to leverage the full power of Flowise AI in a way that is both flexible and customized to your specific application requirements.

3.2.2 Creating Custom Nodes Using Code

While built-in nodes offer robust functionality, there are times when your application demands custom behavior that goes beyond the standard configurations. Creating custom nodes using code allows you to extend the platform's capabilities and implement specialized logic tailored to your unique requirements. This section explains how to develop, integrate, and deploy custom nodes within Flowise AI.

Steps to Create a Custom Node

- **1. Define Your Custom Functionality:**
  Begin by identifying the specific operation or transformation that the built-in nodes cannot provide. This might include complex data manipulations, integrations with external services, or unique processing logic.
- **2. Create a Custom Function:**
  Write a standalone function in your preferred programming language (typically Python) that encapsulates the desired behavior. For example, if you want to create a node that transforms text into title case, your function might look like this:

```python
Copy code
def to_title_case(text):
    return text.title()
```

- **3. Develop a Custom Node Class:**
  To integrate your function into the Flowise AI environment, create a custom node class by inheriting from Flowise AI's base node class. Implement required methods such as initialization and data processing. For example:

```python
Copy code
from flowise.nodes import BaseNode

class CustomTitleCaseNode(BaseNode):
    def __init__(self, name="CustomTitleCaseNode"):
        super().__init__(name)
        # Initialize any custom settings if needed

    def process(self, input_data):
        """
        Processes the input text and converts it to
title case.

        Args:
```

```
        input_data (str): The text input to be
transformed.

        Returns:
            str: The transformed text in title case.
        """
        return to_title_case(input_data)

def to_title_case(text):
    return text.title()
```

- **4. Register Your Custom Node:**
  Once the custom node class is defined, register it with the Flowise AI system so it appears in your Node Library. Registration can be done through configuration files or dedicated commands, depending on your setup. This step ensures that the node is available for use just like any built-in node.

Integration and Testing

- **Integration into Workflows:**
  After registration, drag your custom node from the Node Library onto the Visual Workflow Builder. Connect it with other nodes to form part of a larger workflow.
- **Testing and Debugging:**
  - Use simulated inputs to test your custom node in isolation.
  - Monitor outputs via the Log Monitoring system to ensure that your node processes data as intended.
  - Make incremental adjustments to your code based on test feedback to refine the node's behavior.

Best Practices

- **Modular Design:**
  Keep your custom functions and node classes modular. This approach enhances readability and makes maintenance easier.
- **Documentation:**
  Document your custom node's purpose, configuration options, and any external dependencies. Clear documentation is invaluable for future updates and for other developers who may use or extend your node.
- **Community Engagement:**
  Share your custom nodes with the Flowise AI community.

Collaborating with others can provide feedback, foster improvements, and contribute to a broader repository of useful extensions.

Summary

Creating custom nodes using code empowers you to extend Flowise AI beyond its built-in capabilities. By defining specific functionality, developing a custom node class, and integrating it into your workflow, you gain the flexibility to tailor the platform to your precise needs. Following best practices in modular design, thorough testing, and clear documentation will ensure that your custom nodes are robust, maintainable, and valuable additions to your AI development toolkit.

3.3 Advanced Node Library Extensions

Beyond the built-in and custom nodes, Flowise AI offers the opportunity to extend the Node Library through advanced integrations and enhancements. These extensions allow you to incorporate external services, optimize performance, and introduce new functionalities that are not available out of the box. In this section, we explore techniques and strategies for expanding your Node Library, ensuring that your workflows can tackle even more complex and specialized tasks.

Integration with External APIs and Services

- **Seamless Connectivity:**
  Enhance your workflows by integrating with third-party APIs. Whether it's connecting to external databases, accessing specialized data sources, or utilizing advanced AI services, external integrations enable you to enrich your workflows with additional data and functionality.
- **Dynamic Data Retrieval:**
  Utilize extension nodes that are designed to fetch real-time data from external systems. For example, a node can be created to query a weather API, stock market service, or social media platform, and then feed that information into subsequent processing nodes.
- **Custom Middleware:**
  Develop middleware nodes that act as bridges between Flowise AI and external systems. These nodes can transform data formats,

manage authentication, and handle error responses, ensuring a smooth integration process.

Performance Optimization Techniques

- **Parallel Processing:**
  Extend the Node Library with nodes that support parallel execution. By designing nodes to handle concurrent processing, you can significantly reduce the overall execution time of complex workflows.
- **Resource Management:**
  Implement advanced nodes that monitor resource usage and adjust workload distribution in real time. These nodes can help optimize memory and CPU usage, particularly in large-scale deployments.
- **Caching and Preprocessing:**
  Create extension nodes that incorporate caching mechanisms to store frequently accessed data. This reduces the need for repetitive API calls or heavy computations, leading to faster and more efficient workflows.

Custom Extensions and Plugin Development

- **Modular Plugin Architecture:**
  Flowise AI supports a plugin-based system where developers can create extensions that are easily added or removed from the Node Library. This modularity ensures that custom functionalities can be integrated without disrupting existing workflows.
- **Community-Contributed Extensions:**
  Leverage the collective expertise of the Flowise AI community by exploring and adopting community-contributed plugins. These extensions often address common challenges and provide innovative solutions that have been tested in real-world scenarios.
- **Version Control and Upgradability:**
  Ensure that your custom extensions are maintainable by following best practices for version control. Modular extensions allow for seamless updates and iterative improvements without impacting the overall stability of your workflows.

Testing and Quality Assurance

- **Robust Testing Frameworks:**
  Integrate unit testing and performance benchmarking within your custom extensions. This proactive approach helps catch issues early and ensures that new nodes perform reliably under varying loads.
- **Iterative Feedback and Optimization:**
  Use iterative development cycles to refine advanced node extensions. Collect feedback from logs, performance metrics, and user experiences to continually optimize and enhance the capabilities of your extensions.

Summary

Advanced Node Library Extensions empower you to push the boundaries of what Flowise AI can do. By integrating external APIs, optimizing performance through parallel processing and caching, and developing modular plugins, you can customize the platform to meet highly specialized requirements. These extensions not only enhance the functionality and efficiency of your workflows but also pave the way for innovative applications that leverage the full potential of modern AI technologies. As you continue to develop and deploy your workflows, exploring advanced extensions will be key to maintaining a robust, scalable, and adaptable AI solution.

3.3.1 Integrating External APIs

Integrating external APIs into Flowise AI workflows expands the platform's capabilities by connecting it with external data sources and specialized services. This integration allows your workflows to fetch real-time data, incorporate advanced processing functions, and interact with third-party platforms seamlessly. Here's how you can leverage external APIs within Flowise AI:

Key Considerations for API Integration

- **Authentication and Security:**
  - Ensure secure connections by configuring authentication methods such as API keys, OAuth tokens, or certificates.
  - Store sensitive credentials securely, often using environment variables or secure configuration files.

- **Data Formats and Protocols:**
  - APIs typically exchange data in formats like JSON or XML. Verify that your nodes can parse and process these formats.
  - Adhere to standard protocols (e.g., HTTPS) to maintain data integrity and security.
- **Error Handling and Rate Limiting:**
  - Implement robust error handling to gracefully manage issues such as timeouts, network errors, or rate limits imposed by external services.
  - Design your workflow to retry failed requests or fallback to cached data when necessary.

Steps to Integrate an External API

1. **Identify the API Endpoint:**
   - Determine the API service you wish to integrate (e.g., weather data, stock market updates, social media feeds) and review its documentation for available endpoints and required parameters.
2. **Create a Custom or Extension Node:**
   - Develop a node dedicated to interfacing with the API. This node should handle sending requests and parsing responses.
   - Example (Python snippet):

```python
Copy code
import requests

def fetch_data_from_api(api_url, params, headers):
    response = requests.get(api_url, params=params, headers=headers)
    if response.status_code == 200:
        return response.json()
    else:
        # Handle errors or retry logic here
        return None
```

3. **Configure Node Properties:**
   - In the Properties Panel, set up configurable fields for the API URL, authentication details, and any required parameters.
   - Provide default values or sample configurations to simplify initial testing.
4. **Test API Communication:**

- o Run your custom node in isolation with simulated inputs to ensure it correctly fetches and processes data from the external API.
- o Monitor logs for any errors or performance issues during the API call.

5. **Integrate into a Larger Workflow:**
   - o Once tested, incorporate the API node into your workflow, connecting it with other nodes (e.g., processing nodes to transform the fetched data or output nodes to display results).

Best Practices for API Integration

- **Modular Design:**
  Create the API integration as a self-contained node or plugin, making it reusable across different workflows without duplicating code.
- **Caching Responses:**
  To improve performance and reduce the number of API calls, consider implementing caching strategies for frequently requested data.
- **Documentation and Maintenance:**
  Keep detailed documentation of your API integration, including configuration parameters and error-handling procedures. Regularly update your integration to adapt to any changes in the external API's specifications.

Summary

Integrating external APIs within Flowise AI unlocks a new dimension of functionality by bridging the platform with real-time, specialized data and services. By focusing on secure authentication, robust error handling, and modular node design, you can build resilient and flexible workflows that capitalize on the strengths of external APIs. This approach not only enriches your data processing capabilities but also enables you to build more dynamic, context-aware AI applications.

3.3.2 Performance Optimization Techniques

Enhancing the performance of your workflows is crucial when working with complex AI systems. Performance optimization ensures that your workflows run efficiently, reducing execution time, managing resource usage, and scaling effectively. In this section, we explore various strategies and techniques to optimize performance within Flowise AI.

Parallel Processing and Concurrency

- **Concurrent Execution:**
  Design nodes to operate in parallel where possible. This reduces the overall processing time by allowing independent nodes to execute simultaneously.
- **Task Decomposition:**
  Break down complex tasks into smaller, independent subtasks that can be distributed across multiple nodes. This approach can improve throughput and leverage multi-core processor capabilities.

Resource Management

- **Memory and CPU Optimization:**
  Monitor and fine-tune the memory and CPU usage of nodes. Adjust parameters such as batch sizes or processing intervals to prevent resource bottlenecks.
- **Load Balancing:**
  Distribute workloads evenly across available resources. Implementing load balancing strategies within your workflows can help avoid overloading specific nodes.

Caching and Data Reuse

- **Caching Mechanisms:**
  Implement caching strategies to store intermediate results or frequently accessed data. This reduces the need for repeated computations or API calls, thereby saving time.
- **Data Preprocessing:**
  Preprocess data to minimize on-the-fly transformations during runtime. Precomputed data can speed up processing, especially in repetitive or high-frequency tasks.

Asynchronous Operations

- **Non-Blocking Calls:**
  Use asynchronous programming techniques for operations that involve waiting on external resources (e.g., API requests or database queries). Non-blocking operations help maintain workflow responsiveness.

- **Event-Driven Triggers:**
  Configure nodes to react to specific events or data conditions rather than executing on a fixed schedule, which can enhance efficiency.

Profiling and Monitoring

- **Performance Metrics:**
  Utilize profiling tools to measure execution times, memory consumption, and throughput of individual nodes and entire workflows. Identifying bottlenecks is the first step to optimization.
- **Real-Time Monitoring:**
  Leverage the built-in Log Monitoring and Console tools in Flowise AI to track performance metrics in real time. This enables you to quickly identify and address performance issues during development and production.

Code and Algorithm Optimization

- **Efficient Algorithms:**
  Review and optimize the underlying algorithms used within your nodes. Even small improvements in algorithm efficiency can result in significant performance gains when processing large datasets.
- **Refactoring and Code Review:**
  Regularly refactor your custom code for clarity and efficiency. Peer reviews can help identify inefficiencies or redundant operations that could be optimized.

Scalability Considerations

- **Containerization and Orchestration:**
  When deploying workflows in production, use containerization (e.g., Docker) and orchestration tools (e.g., Kubernetes) to automatically scale resources based on workload demands.
- **Horizontal Scaling:**
  Design your workflows to support horizontal scaling. This allows you to add more nodes or distribute tasks across multiple instances as the demand increases.

Summary

Performance optimization in Flowise AI involves a combination of strategies aimed at reducing processing time, managing resource usage efficiently, and ensuring scalability. By implementing parallel processing, leveraging caching mechanisms, adopting asynchronous operations, and continuously monitoring performance metrics, you can significantly enhance the efficiency of your AI workflows. These optimization techniques not only improve the user experience but also ensure that your workflows remain robust and responsive as they scale to meet increasing demands.

Chapter 4: Integrating with LLM Frameworks

4.1 Overview of Large Language Models in AI

Large Language Models (LLMs) represent one of the most transformative innovations in artificial intelligence over the past decade. These models are designed to process, understand, and generate human-like text by learning from vast amounts of data. In this section, we provide an overview of LLMs, covering their evolution, capabilities, and the role they play in modern AI applications.

Evolution of LLMs

- **Early Developments:**
  LLMs evolved from simpler statistical language models to sophisticated neural architectures. Early models focused on n-gram approaches that predicted text based on limited context, while later developments shifted toward deep learning, enabling more nuanced and context-aware text generation.
- **Breakthrough with Neural Networks:**
  The advent of neural network architectures, particularly the transformer model introduced in 2017, marked a turning point. This architecture allowed models to capture long-range dependencies in text, dramatically improving their performance on various language tasks.
- **Scaling Up:**
  Recent models, such as OpenAI's GPT series, Google's BERT, and subsequent iterations, have pushed the boundaries by training on billions of words. These models leverage extensive datasets and massive computational resources, resulting in capabilities that range from generating creative content to performing complex language understanding tasks.

Capabilities and Applications

- **Text Generation and Completion:**
  LLMs can generate coherent and contextually relevant text based on given prompts. This ability is leveraged in applications such as content creation, chatbots, and automated report generation.

- **Language Understanding and Summarization:**
  Beyond text generation, LLMs excel at comprehending and summarizing large bodies of text. This makes them valuable for tasks like document summarization, translation, and sentiment analysis.
- **Contextual Adaptability:**
  LLMs are fine-tunable for specific tasks or domains. By adjusting the models on domain-specific data, developers can enhance the relevance and accuracy of the outputs, tailoring the model's behavior to specialized applications.
- **Interactive AI Systems:**
  The conversational capabilities of LLMs have paved the way for more interactive AI systems. They enable natural language interfaces where users can have meaningful, context-rich dialogues with machines, improving user experiences in customer support, virtual assistants, and educational tools.

LLMs in Modern AI Ecosystem

- **Integration with Other Technologies:**
  In platforms like Flowise AI, LLMs are integrated as specialized nodes that interface seamlessly with other components. This allows developers to combine generative capabilities with data retrieval (as seen in RAG systems) and orchestrate complex workflows that leverage multiple AI modalities.
- **Continuous Advancements:**
  The field of LLMs is rapidly evolving. Researchers and developers are constantly working on improving model efficiency, reducing biases, and ensuring that outputs are both accurate and ethical. These ongoing advancements ensure that LLMs remain at the forefront of AI innovation.

Summary

Large Language Models have revolutionized how machines understand and generate human language. Their evolution from basic statistical models to advanced neural networks has unlocked a wide range of applications, from creative content generation to precise language comprehension. In the context of Flowise AI, LLMs serve as powerful building blocks, enabling developers to craft intelligent, context-aware workflows that meet modern AI challenges. As you explore further into this book, you will see practical examples of how to integrate and fine-tune LLMs to create advanced AI applications that are both robust and scalable.

4.2 Integrating Popular LLMs

Integrating popular Large Language Models (LLMs) into Flowise AI allows developers to harness the power of advanced natural language processing without starting from scratch. This section outlines strategies and examples for incorporating well-known LLMs—such as OpenAI's GPT series, Google's BERT, and other emerging models—into your workflows.

Key Considerations

- **API Access and Licensing:**
  - Many popular LLMs are available via APIs (e.g., OpenAI's API for GPT models). Ensure you have the necessary credentials, understand usage limits, and are compliant with licensing agreements.
- **Model Selection:**
  - Choose the LLM that best suits your application requirements. For instance, GPT models are ideal for generating creative and conversational text, while BERT-based models excel in understanding context for tasks like classification or summarization.
- **Configuration and Fine-Tuning:**
  - Most LLMs offer configurable parameters such as temperature, max tokens, and prompt engineering. Fine-tuning these settings in Flowise AI nodes can help tailor the model's outputs to your specific use case.

Integration Steps

1. **Obtain API Credentials:**
   - Sign up for access to your chosen LLM service (e.g., OpenAI, Hugging Face, etc.).
   - Secure your API key and store it in a secure manner (e.g., using environment variables).
2. **Set Up an LLM Node in Flowise AI:**
   - **Create a dedicated LLM node:**
     Use Flowise AI's built-in or custom node system to create a node that will handle requests to the LLM API.
   - **Configure the Node:**
     In the Properties Panel, specify parameters such as:
     - API endpoint URL

- Authentication headers (e.g., API key)
- Prompt template or input data
- Model-specific settings like temperature, maximum tokens, and stop sequences

3. **Implement a Code Example:**
   - Here's a simple Python snippet that illustrates how you might integrate an LLM via API within a custom Flowise AI node:

```python
Copy code
import requests

def call_gpt_api(prompt, api_key, model="text-
davinci-003", max_tokens=150, temperature=0.7):
    url = "https://api.openai.com/v1/completions"
    headers = {
        "Content-Type": "application/json",
        "Authorization": f"Bearer {api_key}"
    }
    payload = {
        "model": model,
        "prompt": prompt,
        "max_tokens": max_tokens,
        "temperature": temperature
    }
    response = requests.post(url,
headers=headers, json=payload)
    if response.status_code == 200:
        return
response.json().get("choices")[0].get("text").str
ip()
    else:
        # Handle errors gracefully
        return f"Error: {response.status_code} -
{response.text}"

# Example usage:
api_key = "YOUR_API_KEY_HERE"
prompt = "Explain the benefits of integrating
LLMs into AI workflows."
result = call_gpt_api(prompt, api_key)
print("LLM Output:", result)
```

   - **Explanation:**
   This code sends a prompt to OpenAI's GPT API and retrieves the generated text. In a Flowise AI node, similar logic can be encapsulated and configured via the node's properties.

73

4. **Integrate with Workflow:**
   - Connect the LLM node to other nodes within the Visual Workflow Builder. For example, use an Input node to capture user queries, pass the query to the LLM node, and then route the generated output to an Output node or further processing nodes.
   - Use simulated inputs for testing, then gradually integrate real-time data as the workflow stabilizes.

Best Practices

- **Prompt Engineering:**
  Experiment with different prompt formats to guide the LLM towards generating the desired output. Small changes in phrasing can significantly affect the response quality.
- **Error Handling:**
  Implement fallback mechanisms such as default responses or retries when API calls fail, ensuring that your workflow remains robust.
- **Performance Monitoring:**
  Monitor response times and usage metrics through integrated logging and performance tools within Flowise AI. This helps optimize parameters and manage costs effectively.
- **Modular Design:**
  Design your LLM integration as a reusable node that can be easily plugged into different workflows. This promotes consistency and reduces duplication of code.

Summary

Integrating popular LLMs into Flowise AI enables you to leverage advanced language generation and comprehension capabilities with minimal overhead. By obtaining API credentials, configuring dedicated LLM nodes, and fine-tuning model parameters, you can seamlessly incorporate models like GPT and BERT into your workflows. The strategies and examples provided here offer a roadmap to building intelligent, responsive AI applications that harness the latest advancements in natural language processing.

4.2.1 OpenAI GPT, BERT, and Other Models

The landscape of Large Language Models (LLMs) includes several prominent architectures, each with its own strengths and specialized applications. In this section, we focus on three key players: OpenAI's GPT series, Google's BERT, and other emerging models, outlining their core characteristics, typical use cases, and how they can be integrated within Flowise AI workflows.

OpenAI GPT Series

- **Architecture and Capabilities:**
  The GPT (Generative Pre-trained Transformer) series is designed primarily for text generation. These models leverage a transformer architecture that excels in understanding context and producing coherent, human-like text. They are particularly adept at generating creative content, answering questions, and engaging in conversational tasks.
- **Common Use Cases:**
    o Content creation (articles, summaries, creative writing)
    o Chatbots and virtual assistants
    o Interactive conversational agents
    o Automated customer support
- **Integration Considerations:**
    o Access via OpenAI API with proper authentication and parameter tuning (e.g., temperature, max tokens).
    o Ideal for workflows where dynamic text generation is needed, and where prompt engineering plays a crucial role in guiding responses.

Google's BERT

- **Architecture and Capabilities:**
  BERT (Bidirectional Encoder Representations from Transformers) is designed primarily for understanding context within text rather than generating new text. It uses a bidirectional approach, processing text from both left-to-right and right-to-left, which enables it to capture nuanced meanings and relationships within language.
- **Common Use Cases:**
    o Text classification and sentiment analysis
    o Named entity recognition and question answering
    o Document summarization and information retrieval

o   Enhancing search algorithms
- **Integration Considerations:**
    o   Often used as part of a fine-tuning process for specific tasks.
    o   Can be integrated into workflows that require accurate comprehension of text, providing a foundation for downstream tasks like classification or data extraction.

Other Emerging Models

- **Diverse Architectures:**
  Beyond GPT and BERT, the AI community has seen a surge in alternative LLMs designed for specific purposes or optimized for efficiency. Examples include models like T5 (Text-to-Text Transfer Transformer) and newer variants offered through platforms such as Hugging Face.
- **Specialized Capabilities:**
    o   **T5:** Converts every NLP problem into a text-to-text format, making it highly versatile for tasks ranging from translation to summarization.
    o   **Smaller, Optimized Models:** Recent developments also focus on creating lightweight models that offer faster inference times and lower resource requirements, making them suitable for edge deployments or real-time applications.
- **Integration Considerations:**
    o   Choice of model should be based on the specific requirements of your workflow—whether the need is for text generation, comprehension, or a combination of both.
    o   Many of these models are accessible via open-source libraries and APIs, providing flexibility in deployment and customization.

Integrating These Models in Flowise AI

Flowise AI provides dedicated nodes to interact with these models, allowing you to:

- **Select the Appropriate Node:** Choose between nodes configured for text generation (ideal for GPT) or text understanding (optimized for BERT or similar models).
- **Configure Model Parameters:** Set model-specific parameters through the Properties Panel, such as prompt design for GPT nodes or fine-tuning settings for BERT-based nodes.

- **Combine Models:** Leverage a hybrid approach where outputs from BERT (e.g., classification results) feed into GPT nodes to generate enriched, context-aware responses. This is particularly useful in applications like intelligent customer support where understanding and generation are both essential.

Summary

OpenAI's GPT, Google's BERT, and other emerging LLMs each bring distinct advantages to the table. GPT models excel in generating human-like text, making them ideal for creative and conversational applications, while BERT is better suited for deep text understanding and classification tasks. Additionally, emerging models like T5 offer versatile, text-to-text solutions. By understanding the strengths of these models and integrating them appropriately within Flowise AI, you can build sophisticated workflows that leverage the best of modern natural language processing technology.

4.2.2 Fine-Tuning and Customizing LLMs for Specific Tasks

Fine-tuning LLMs tailors a pre-trained model to excel at a particular task or domain, enhancing performance and accuracy. This process involves adjusting the model's parameters using domain-specific datasets so that the output is more relevant and precise for your application. Here's how to approach fine-tuning and customization:

Understanding Fine-Tuning

- **Purpose:**
  Fine-tuning bridges the gap between a general-purpose language model and the specific needs of your project. It helps the model learn the nuances of specialized terminology, context, and style that are essential for tasks like customer support, legal document analysis, or technical content generation.
- **Process Overview:**
  Fine-tuning typically involves:
  - ○ **Dataset Preparation:** Curate a dataset that reflects the target domain, ensuring it is labeled or structured according to the desired output.
  - ○ **Training:** Adjust the model's weights on the new dataset using transfer learning techniques while keeping most pre-trained knowledge intact.

o **Evaluation and Iteration:** Test the fine-tuned model on validation datasets and iterate on the training process to achieve optimal performance.

Customizing LLMs in Flowise AI

Flowise AI supports integration with fine-tuned models, enabling you to incorporate custom LLMs into your workflows. Here's how to configure and customize LLMs for specific tasks:

- **Select a Base Model:**
  Begin with a robust pre-trained model such as GPT, BERT, or T5, depending on whether your task involves text generation, comprehension, or a mix of both.
- **Prepare Your Dataset:**
  Collect and preprocess data relevant to your domain. Ensure that your dataset is clean, balanced, and representative of the scenarios your model will encounter.
- **Fine-Tuning Process:**
  o **Local Fine-Tuning:** You can fine-tune models using libraries like Hugging Face's Transformers, which provide utilities to adapt models on your custom dataset.
  o **API-Based Customization:** Some platforms (e.g., OpenAI) offer fine-tuning options directly through their APIs, allowing you to upload your dataset and receive a customized model.
- **Integrate the Fine-Tuned Model:**
  Once fine-tuning is complete, deploy the customized model within Flowise AI. Configure the LLM node with the appropriate endpoint, authentication details, and any new parameters that came with the fine-tuned version.
- **Model-Specific Parameters:**
  Adjust settings such as temperature, maximum tokens, and prompt format in the Properties Panel to ensure that the fine-tuned model's output aligns with your expectations. Fine-tuning often reduces the need for extensive prompt engineering, as the model is now more aligned with your domain.

Best Practices

- **Continuous Evaluation:**
  Monitor the performance of the fine-tuned model on real-world data.

Regularly evaluate its outputs and update the training dataset as needed to maintain high accuracy and relevance.

- **Iterative Training:**
  Fine-tuning is rarely a one-off process. Use an iterative approach to gradually improve the model's performance by incorporating new data and feedback.
- **Resource Management:**
  Fine-tuning large models can be resource-intensive. Utilize cloud-based GPU services if local hardware is limited, and consider the cost-performance trade-offs.
- **Documentation and Version Control:**
  Maintain detailed documentation of your fine-tuning process, including dataset characteristics, training parameters, and performance metrics. This practice helps in troubleshooting and ensures reproducibility.

Summary

Fine-tuning and customizing LLMs enable you to harness the full potential of language models by adapting them to your specific needs. By selecting the right base model, preparing a quality dataset, and iteratively fine-tuning, you can significantly enhance the model's performance for specialized tasks. Flowise AI's flexible integration capabilities make it easy to deploy these customized models, ensuring that your workflows deliver precise, context-aware outputs tailored to your domain.

4.3 Practical Workflow Examples

In this section, we illustrate how to apply the integration of LLMs within Flowise AI through a variety of real-world workflow examples. These examples demonstrate how LLMs can be leveraged to automate tasks, enhance user interactions, and generate valuable insights. Each example is designed to highlight different aspects of LLM integration, from generating conversational responses to summarizing large documents.

Example 1: Intelligent Chatbot Workflow

- **Objective:**
  Create a conversational chatbot that responds to user inquiries using a fine-tuned GPT model.
- **Workflow Components:**

- o **Input Node:** Captures user text input from a chat interface.
- o **LLM Node (GPT):** Processes the input and generates a human-like response.
- o **Processing Node:** Optionally refines the generated text (e.g., filtering inappropriate content or applying additional formatting).
- o **Output Node:** Displays the chatbot's response on the user interface.
- **Key Considerations:**
  - o Utilize prompt engineering to steer responses toward being informative and polite.
  - o Implement error handling to manage API failures or unexpected outputs.
- **Workflow Flow:**

  0. **User Query:** User submits a question.
  1. **LLM Processing:** The query is forwarded to the LLM node which generates a response using the GPT API.
  2. **Post-Processing:** The generated response is further processed if needed.
  3. **Display Output:** The final response is displayed to the user.

Example 2: Document Summarization

- **Objective:**
  Summarize long documents or reports into concise summaries that capture the key points.
- **Workflow Components:**
  - o **Input Node:** Ingests a full-length document from a file or an online source.
  - o **Preprocessing Node:** Cleans and segments the document into manageable parts.
  - o **LLM Node (e.g., GPT or T5):** Processes the segmented text to generate summaries.
  - o **Aggregation Node:** Combines individual summaries into a cohesive final summary.
  - o **Output Node:** Displays or stores the summarized content.
- **Key Considerations:**
  - o Fine-tune the LLM on summarization tasks if needed.
  - o Manage token limits by processing the document in sections.

- **Workflow Flow:**

  0. **Document Input:** The workflow starts with a long text document.
  1. **Segmentation:** The document is split into smaller sections.
  2. **Section Summarization:** Each section is sent to the LLM node to generate a brief summary.
  3. **Summary Aggregation:** The individual summaries are merged into a final cohesive summary.
  4. **Output:** The final summary is provided to the user or stored in a database.

Example 3: Automated Content Generation for Marketing

- **Objective:**
  Generate creative content for marketing campaigns, such as blog posts or social media updates, based on a given topic.
- **Workflow Components:**
  - **Input Node:** Receives a topic or keyword from the user or a pre-defined list.
  - **LLM Node (GPT):** Generates a draft blog post or social media content related to the topic.
  - **Editing Node:** Optionally applies stylistic changes or corrections.
  - **Output Node:** Publishes or saves the generated content.
- **Key Considerations:**
  - Use temperature and max tokens settings to control the creativity and length of the output.
  - Implement iterative feedback loops to refine the content based on user edits.
- **Workflow Flow:**

  0. **Topic Submission:** User inputs a topic (e.g., "Benefits of AI in healthcare").
  1. **Content Generation:** The topic is processed by the LLM node to generate a draft article.
  2. **Content Refinement:** The draft passes through an editing node that refines the text.
  3. **Final Output:** The polished content is either published directly or sent to a review system.

Example 4: Customer Support Response Generation

- **Objective:**
Provide automated, context-aware responses to common customer support queries.
- **Workflow Components:**
    - **Input Node:** Receives a customer query from a support chat interface.
    - **RAG Node:** Retrieves relevant information from a support knowledge base using a Retrieval-Augmented Generation approach.
    - **LLM Node (GPT):** Combines the query and retrieved context to generate a detailed answer.
    - **Output Node:** Delivers the answer back to the customer.
- **Key Considerations:**
    - Ensure that the retrieval component is finely tuned to fetch the most relevant documents.
    - Use prompt templates that merge customer query with contextual data for improved response quality.
- **Workflow Flow:**

    0. **Customer Query:** The customer submits a query, such as "How do I reset my password?"
    1. **Context Retrieval:** A RAG node retrieves the relevant support document or FAQ entry.
    2. **Response Generation:** The LLM node generates a tailored answer by integrating the query with the context.
    3. **Output:** The response is sent back to the customer, providing clear, actionable guidance.

Summary

These practical workflow examples demonstrate how integrating LLMs into Flowise AI can transform diverse applications—from creating interactive chatbots and summarizing documents to generating marketing content and enhancing customer support. Each example emphasizes a tailored approach to meet specific task requirements, showcasing the flexibility and power of Flowise AI when combined with advanced language models. As you explore these workflows, you'll gain insights into configuring nodes, managing data flow, and refining outputs to build robust, real-world AI applications.

4.3.1 Text Generation and Summarization

Text generation and summarization are two key applications of Large Language Models (LLMs) that enable automated creation and refinement of textual content. In Flowise AI, these capabilities are integrated into dedicated workflows that streamline tasks such as drafting creative content and distilling lengthy documents into concise summaries. This section explores both functions, detailing their processes, typical use cases, and implementation strategies within Flowise AI.

Text Generation

- **Purpose and Capabilities:**
  Text generation involves creating coherent, contextually relevant, and human-like text based on given prompts. LLMs, such as those in the GPT series, excel in this area by leveraging vast training data to generate creative narratives, responses, or content drafts.
- **Use Cases:**
  - **Creative Writing:** Generating articles, blog posts, and social media content.
  - **Conversational Agents:** Powering chatbots and virtual assistants that engage users in natural language dialogues.
  - **Automated Reporting:** Producing structured reports or summaries from raw data inputs.
- **Implementation in Flowise AI:**
  - **LLM Node Configuration:** Use a dedicated LLM node where you can input a prompt and configure parameters like temperature, maximum tokens, and response style.
  - **Prompt Engineering:** Design prompts that clearly instruct the model on the desired output, enhancing quality and relevance.
  - **Iterative Refinement:** Incorporate feedback loops and additional processing nodes to polish the generated text if necessary.

Summarization

- **Purpose and Capabilities:**
  Summarization focuses on distilling long-form text into concise,

coherent summaries that capture the essential points. This is particularly valuable for processing extensive documents or reports where users need quick insights.

- **Use Cases:**
  - **Document Summarization:** Creating brief summaries of articles, research papers, or reports.
  - **Customer Support:** Summarizing extensive support logs or knowledge base documents for quick reference.
  - **Data Analysis:** Condensing verbose data outputs into digestible overviews for decision-makers.
- **Implementation in Flowise AI:**
  - **Segmentation and Preprocessing:** Use input nodes to split longer documents into manageable sections.
  - **LLM or Specialized Summarization Nodes:** Deploy nodes that specifically apply summarization techniques, whether by fine-tuning an LLM for this task or using a model like T5 designed for text-to-text tasks.
  - **Aggregation of Summaries:** Combine individual section summaries into a cohesive final summary using an aggregation node.

Workflow Integration

- **Seamless Data Flow:**
  Integrate text generation and summarization nodes into broader workflows where outputs from one process feed into another. For example, generate initial content using a text generation node and then use a summarization node to create an executive summary.
- **Customization and Fine-Tuning:**
  Adjust parameters and incorporate custom code in nodes to tailor outputs to specific domain requirements. This includes tuning the model's creativity for generation or ensuring that summaries retain key information from the source text.

Summary

Text generation and summarization are powerful functions enabled by LLMs, and Flowise AI makes their integration straightforward. By configuring dedicated nodes, employing effective prompt engineering, and establishing efficient workflows, developers can automate the creation of engaging content and distill lengthy texts into concise summaries. These capabilities not only improve productivity but also enhance user interaction and decision-making across various applications.

4.3.2 Chatbot Implementation

Implementing a chatbot is one of the most popular and practical applications of Large Language Models (LLMs) in Flowise AI. By leveraging LLMs' natural language processing capabilities, you can create interactive, context-aware chatbots that engage users, provide support, and automate routine tasks. This section outlines the components, workflow design, and best practices for building a chatbot within Flowise AI.

Key Components of a Chatbot Workflow

- **Input Node:**
  Captures user messages from a chat interface. This node is responsible for collecting queries or conversational prompts from users.
- **LLM Node (e.g., GPT-based):**
  Processes user inputs using a pre-trained or fine-tuned language model. The LLM node generates a response based on the input prompt and any additional context provided.
- **Processing Node:**
  Optionally refines the generated text. This may include filtering inappropriate language, formatting the response, or integrating additional logic to tailor the output.
- **Contextual or RAG Node (Optional):**
  For more advanced implementations, incorporate a Retrieval-Augmented Generation (RAG) node. This node retrieves relevant documents or data (e.g., FAQs, support articles) to enrich the response, ensuring accuracy and context.
- **Output Node:**
  Delivers the final response back to the user through the chat interface. This node ensures that the response is displayed in a user-friendly format.

Designing the Chatbot Workflow

1. **User Interaction:**

- o The conversation starts when a user submits a query via the chat interface.
- o The Input Node captures the query and passes it along to the LLM node.

2. **Generating a Response:**
- o The LLM Node receives the query and, using prompt engineering techniques, generates a draft response.
- o If integrated, the RAG Node can fetch contextually relevant information from a knowledge base, which is merged with the draft response to enhance accuracy.

3. **Post-Processing:**
- o The Processing Node may further modify the text. This could involve formatting the response, removing any undesired content, or applying domain-specific rules.

4. **Delivering the Answer:**
- o The final, refined response is sent to the Output Node, which displays the message in the chat interface.

Sample Code Example

Below is a simplified Python-like pseudocode example illustrating the core logic behind a chatbot workflow:

```python
Copy code
# Example function to simulate a chatbot response using an
LLM API
import requests

def generate_chat_response(user_query, api_key):
    # Define the prompt for the LLM node
    prompt = f"User: {user_query}\nChatbot:"

    # API call to an LLM (e.g., OpenAI GPT)
    response = requests.post(
        "https://api.openai.com/v1/completions",
        headers={
            "Content-Type": "application/json",
            "Authorization": f"Bearer {api_key}"
        },
        json={
            "model": "text-davinci-003",
            "prompt": prompt,
            "max_tokens": 100,
            "temperature": 0.7
        }
```

```
    )
    if response.status_code == 200:
        return response.json()["choices"][0]["text"].strip()
    else:
        return "I'm sorry, but I couldn't process your
request right now."

# Simulate the chatbot workflow
def chatbot_workflow(user_query, api_key):
    # Step 1: Input Node captures the query
    captured_query = user_query  # (In practice, this is
provided by the chat interface)

    # Step 2: LLM Node generates a draft response
    draft_response = generate_chat_response(captured_query,
api_key)

    # Step 3: Processing Node refines the response (optional)
    refined_response = draft_response  # Here, additional
processing could be applied

    # Step 4: Output Node delivers the final response
    return refined_response

# Example usage
api_key = "YOUR_API_KEY"
user_query = "How can I reset my password?"
final_response = chatbot_workflow(user_query, api_key)
print("Chatbot Response:", final_response)
```

Best Practices for Chatbot Implementation

- **Prompt Engineering:**
  Carefully design prompts to guide the LLM towards producing relevant, friendly, and clear responses. Experiment with prompt variations to improve response quality.
- **Error Handling:**
  Implement robust error handling at each stage of the workflow. For instance, if the LLM node fails to generate a response, the system should provide a default fallback message.
- **Context Management:**
  For multi-turn conversations, consider maintaining context across exchanges. You can achieve this by appending previous conversation snippets to the prompt or integrating a dedicated context management node.
- **User Feedback Loop:**
  Allow users to provide feedback on responses. This feedback can be

used to iteratively improve the chatbot's performance and fine-tune the underlying LLM.

- **Performance Monitoring:**
  Use Flowise AI's logging and monitoring tools to track response times, error rates, and user interactions. Regular monitoring helps identify bottlenecks and optimize resource usage.

Summary

Chatbot implementation in Flowise AI combines the power of LLMs with a structured, modular workflow design. By capturing user input, generating dynamic responses with an LLM node, optionally enriching responses with external context, and delivering refined output, you can build an interactive and intelligent chatbot. The integration of best practices such as prompt engineering, error handling, and context management ensures that your chatbot is robust, user-friendly, and capable of handling real-world queries effectively.

4.4 Best Practices for LLM Integration

Integrating Large Language Models (LLMs) effectively into your workflows requires careful planning and fine-tuning to ensure that the models operate reliably and deliver high-quality outputs. Here are some best practices to consider when integrating LLMs within Flowise AI:

1. Model Selection and Configuration

- **Choose the Right Model:**
  Select an LLM that best fits your use case. For instance, GPT models are ideal for creative text generation and conversational tasks, whereas BERT-based models excel at text understanding and classification.
- **Configure Model Parameters:**
  Fine-tune settings such as temperature, maximum tokens, and prompt length in the Properties Panel. Adjust these parameters to control the creativity, response length, and specificity of the outputs.

2. Prompt Engineering

- **Craft Clear Prompts:**
  Develop precise prompts that clearly convey the task at hand. Well-

constructed prompts can guide the model to generate more accurate
and relevant responses.

- **Iterate and Test:**
Experiment with different prompt formulations to find the optimal
structure for your application. Use A/B testing with simulated inputs
to evaluate and refine your prompts.

3. Handling Context and Continuity

- **Maintain Conversation History:**
For chatbots or multi-turn dialogues, keep track of conversation
history to provide context for the LLM. This can be achieved by
appending previous interactions to the prompt.
- **Dynamic Context Management:**
Implement nodes or middleware that intelligently select and manage
relevant context, ensuring that the LLM always has access to the
most pertinent information without overwhelming it with excessive
details.

4. Error Handling and Fallback Strategies

- **Implement Robust Error Handling:**
Design workflows to catch and handle API errors, timeouts, or
unexpected responses gracefully. Provide fallback responses or
default outputs to maintain a smooth user experience.
- **Retry Mechanisms:**
Set up automatic retries for transient errors and monitor failure rates
to determine when alternative strategies (like switching models)
might be necessary.

5. Security and Compliance

- **Secure API Credentials:**
Always store API keys and tokens securely using environment
variables or secure configuration files. Avoid hardcoding sensitive
information in your workflows.
- **Data Privacy:**
Ensure that data passed to LLMs complies with privacy regulations,
especially if you're processing personal or sensitive information.

6. Performance Optimization

- **Monitor Response Times:**
  Utilize Flowise AI's monitoring tools to track the performance of LLM nodes. Identify bottlenecks and adjust parameters to optimize throughput and latency.
- **Optimize Costs:**
  Be mindful of the cost implications associated with API calls. Optimize your prompts and node configurations to minimize unnecessary requests while maintaining output quality.

7. Continuous Improvement and Feedback

- **Collect User Feedback:**
  Implement mechanisms to capture user feedback on the outputs generated by the LLM. This feedback can guide future adjustments and refinements.
- **Iterative Updates:**
  Treat LLM integration as an ongoing process. Regularly update and fine-tune your configurations and prompt strategies based on new insights and evolving requirements.

Summary

Integrating LLMs effectively within Flowise AI is not a one-time task but an iterative process that involves careful model selection, precise prompt engineering, robust error handling, and continuous performance monitoring. By following these best practices, you can create reliable, secure, and high-performing AI workflows that leverage the full potential of modern LLMs to deliver engaging and contextually accurate outputs.

Chapter 5: Building Retrieval-Augmented Generation (RAG) Systems

5.1 Fundamentals of RAG Systems

Retrieval-Augmented Generation (RAG) systems represent a hybrid approach that combines the strengths of generative language models with powerful data retrieval mechanisms. This fusion enhances the factual accuracy and contextual relevance of generated outputs by grounding them in external, up-to-date information. In this section, we explore the core principles and components that underpin RAG systems, as well as their advantages and key challenges.

Key Concepts in RAG Systems

- **Dual-Component Structure:**
  RAG systems consist of two primary components:
  - **Retriever:** This component is responsible for fetching relevant documents or data from an external knowledge base, database, or document store based on a given query.
  - **Generator (LLM):** The generative model then takes the retrieved data as context along with the original query to produce more informed and context-aware outputs.
- **Contextual Grounding:**
  By providing the generative model with additional external context, RAG systems help mitigate issues like hallucinations—where a model might generate plausible but incorrect information. The retrieved documents serve as an anchoring mechanism, ensuring that outputs are not solely based on pre-trained data but also reflect current and accurate knowledge.
- **Dynamic Integration:**
  Unlike static models that rely only on fixed training data, RAG systems dynamically integrate fresh information. This makes them especially useful in domains where data changes frequently, such as news, finance, or customer support.

Operational Workflow

1. **Query Processing:**
   The process begins when a query or input is provided. The system uses this query to search for relevant data in an external repository.
2. **Retrieval Phase:**
   The Retriever component identifies and extracts documents or data snippets that are contextually related to the query. This retrieval is typically based on similarity metrics or semantic search algorithms.
3. **Generation Phase:**
   The retrieved data is then fed into the Generator, which uses it alongside the original query to generate a response. The integration of retrieved content ensures that the response is both coherent and anchored in real, verifiable information.
4. **Post-Processing (Optional):**
   Depending on the application, additional processing steps might refine the output—such as formatting, summarization, or further validation against additional data sources.

Advantages of RAG Systems

- **Improved Accuracy:**
  The combination of retrieval and generation enhances the reliability of outputs by incorporating current, context-specific information.
- **Enhanced Relevance:**
  RAG systems can produce more targeted responses, as the retriever helps focus the generative model on pertinent content.
- **Flexibility in Dynamic Environments:**
  They adapt well to rapidly changing information landscapes, making them suitable for real-time applications and environments where up-to-date information is crucial.

Challenges and Considerations

- **Retriever Quality:**
  The overall performance of a RAG system is highly dependent on the effectiveness of the retriever. Poor retrieval quality can lead to irrelevant or inaccurate context, undermining the generator's performance.

- **Latency:**
  Adding a retrieval phase can introduce additional latency, which must be managed carefully in time-sensitive applications.
- **Complexity of Integration:**
  Designing a seamless integration between the retriever and generator requires careful calibration, especially in terms of how retrieved data is formatted and presented to the LLM.

Summary

The fundamentals of RAG systems lie in their ability to merge real-time, contextually relevant information with the generative capabilities of LLMs. This dual approach significantly enhances the accuracy and applicability of AI-generated responses, particularly in dynamic environments where current information is critical. As you build RAG systems within Flowise AI, understanding these core principles will help you design workflows that effectively leverage both retrieval and generation, ensuring robust and reliable AI applications.

5.1.1 Data Retrieval Techniques and Strategies

Data retrieval is a critical component of Retrieval-Augmented Generation (RAG) systems, serving as the foundation for providing context that enhances the accuracy and relevance of generated outputs. This section explores various data retrieval techniques and strategies that can be employed within RAG systems, ensuring that the generator is equipped with high-quality, contextually pertinent information.

Core Data Retrieval Techniques

- **Keyword-Based Search:**
  - **Overview:**
    Traditional keyword search methods rely on matching exact terms from the query with indexed documents.
  - **Techniques:**
    Utilize search algorithms like BM25, which score documents based on term frequency and document length, to rank relevant content.
  - **Strengths and Limitations:**
    This approach is fast and efficient but may miss semantically relevant documents that do not contain the exact keywords.
- **Semantic Search:**

- o **Overview:**
  Semantic search leverages embeddings generated from neural models (e.g., BERT, Sentence Transformers) to capture the underlying meaning of text.
- o **Techniques:**
  Convert both queries and documents into high-dimensional vectors and use similarity measures such as cosine similarity or Euclidean distance to identify relevant content.
- o **Strengths and Limitations:**
  Provides more accurate retrieval by understanding context and intent, though it often requires more computational resources and a well-optimized vector index.
- **Hybrid Search Methods:**
  - o **Overview:**
    Hybrid techniques combine keyword-based and semantic search approaches to balance precision and recall.
  - o **Techniques:**
    Merge scores from both BM25 and semantic similarity metrics, sometimes using re-ranking algorithms to refine the final list of retrieved documents.
  - o **Strengths and Limitations:**
    Offers improved performance by compensating for the weaknesses of each individual method, though integrating these methods requires careful calibration.

Advanced Strategies and Best Practices

- **Query Expansion:**
  Enhance the original query by adding synonyms, related terms, or contextually relevant keywords. This helps in capturing a broader range of documents that might be semantically related to the query.
- **Contextual Filtering:**
  Apply additional filters based on metadata, timestamps, or domain-specific tags to narrow down the search results. This strategy ensures that the retrieved data is not only relevant in content but also appropriate in context.
- **Indexing Optimization:**
  - o **Preprocessing:**
    Clean and preprocess your data (e.g., normalization, removal of stop words) before indexing.
  - o **Advanced Indexing:**
    Use modern indexing solutions such as Elasticsearch for

keyword search or vector databases like FAISS and Pinecone for semantic search, ensuring efficient retrieval even with large datasets.

- **Re-ranking Mechanisms:**
  After initial retrieval, re-rank the results using more sophisticated models that evaluate the contextual relevance of each document. This may involve secondary scoring using neural networks or domain-specific heuristics.
- **Scalability and Latency Considerations:**
  Ensure that your retrieval strategy is optimized for speed, especially in real-time applications. Techniques such as caching frequently accessed results and using distributed search architectures can significantly reduce latency.

Implementation Considerations in RAG Systems

- **Integration with LLMs:**
  The quality of retrieved data directly impacts the performance of the generative model. It is crucial to design retrieval nodes that seamlessly feed into LLM nodes, ensuring that the context provided is formatted correctly and is directly applicable to the generation process.
- **Iterative Refinement:**
  Continuously monitor and refine the retrieval process based on feedback and performance metrics. This may involve tuning similarity thresholds, adjusting re-ranking algorithms, or incorporating new data sources.
- **Robust Error Handling:**
  Implement fallback strategies to handle cases where retrieval yields insufficient or irrelevant results. For example, defaulting to a broader search or providing a generic response can help maintain system reliability.

Summary

Effective data retrieval in RAG systems is achieved through a combination of traditional keyword-based methods, semantic search, and hybrid techniques that integrate the strengths of both approaches. By employing advanced strategies such as query expansion, contextual filtering, optimized indexing, and re-ranking, you can significantly enhance the relevance and quality of the retrieved data. This, in turn, ensures that the generative model produces accurate and contextually enriched outputs, making your RAG system more robust and effective.

5.1.2 Merging Retrieved Data with LLM Outputs

A key challenge in building effective RAG systems is ensuring that the retrieved data meaningfully informs the generated outputs. Merging retrieved data with LLM outputs involves combining the context provided by the retrieval process with the generative capabilities of the language model. This integration enhances the relevance, accuracy, and informativeness of the responses.

Strategies for Merging Data

- **Contextual Prompt Augmentation:**
  - **Incorporate Retrieved Content into Prompts:**
    Embed key excerpts or summarized points from the retrieved data directly into the prompt fed to the LLM.
  - **Template Design:**
    Develop prompt templates that clearly separate the user query from the contextual information, guiding the LLM to use both sources effectively.
- **Dynamic Input Formatting:**
  - **Concatenation Techniques:**
    Combine the original query with the retrieved data into a single prompt while maintaining logical structure.
  - **Weighted Context:**
    Adjust the prominence of the retrieved data relative to the query, ensuring that the LLM prioritizes critical information without overwhelming its generative process.
- **Multi-Step Generation:**
  - **Sequential Processing:**
    First generate a draft response using the query and retrieved context, then refine it by reprocessing the draft with additional instructions.
  - **Iterative Refinement:**
    Use feedback loops where the initial LLM output is re-evaluated in conjunction with the retrieved data to produce a more coherent and factually grounded final response.

Integration Techniques

- **Pre-Processing Nodes:**
  Use pre-processing nodes to clean, format, and summarize the retrieved data before it is merged with the query. This ensures that only the most relevant content is passed to the LLM.
- **LLM Node Configuration:**
  Configure the LLM node to accept multi-part inputs. For example, the prompt can be structured as:

```yaml
Copy code
[User Query]
---
Context:
[Retrieved Data]
---
Answer:
```

This clear delineation helps the model understand the role of each segment in generating the final response.

- **Post-Processing Validation:**
  After merging and generating the output, apply a validation step to ensure that the final response accurately reflects the retrieved context. This might include automated fact-checking or additional processing nodes to highlight key information.

Best Practices

- **Relevance Filtering:**
  Only include the most pertinent information from the retrieved data. Excessive or irrelevant context can confuse the LLM and dilute the quality of the output.
- **Testing and Iteration:**
  Experiment with different merging strategies and prompt structures. Monitor performance using metrics such as accuracy, coherence, and user satisfaction, and refine your approach iteratively.
- **Error Handling:**
  Implement fallback mechanisms in case the retrieved data is insufficient or conflicts with the LLM's output. This might include default responses or prompts to re-fetch additional context.

Summary

Merging retrieved data with LLM outputs is crucial for building robust and context-aware RAG systems. By augmenting prompts with carefully curated retrieved content, employing dynamic formatting techniques, and iteratively refining the outputs, you can significantly enhance the accuracy and relevance of the generated responses. Effective integration not only leverages the strengths of both retrieval and generative components but also ensures that the final output is well-grounded in real, up-to-date information.

5.2 Setting Up and Managing Document Stores

Document stores play a critical role in Retrieval-Augmented Generation (RAG) systems by providing a structured repository for unstructured or semi-structured data. They enable efficient storage, indexing, and retrieval of documents, which serve as contextual anchors for LLM outputs. This section outlines how to set up and manage document stores within Flowise AI, covering key concepts, configuration steps, and best practices.

Key Components and Concepts

- **Definition and Purpose:**
  Document stores are specialized databases designed to handle text, JSON objects, or multimedia files. In a RAG system, they provide the external context by storing relevant documents, articles, or reports that can be queried during the generation process.
- **Indexing and Search:**
  Efficient indexing is crucial for fast retrieval. Document stores typically support:
    - **Keyword-Based Indexing:** Leveraging traditional search algorithms (e.g., BM25) for matching text.
    - **Semantic Indexing:** Utilizing vector embeddings (via models like BERT or Sentence Transformers) to capture contextual similarities.
- **Scalability and Performance:**
  Document stores are built to manage large volumes of data and support quick retrieval even under heavy query loads. They often integrate with distributed systems to ensure high availability and low latency.

Setting Up a Document Store

1. **Choose the Right Database:**
   - o **MongoDB:** A popular NoSQL database that handles JSON-like documents with flexible schema design.
   - o **Elasticsearch:** Ideal for full-text search and complex query capabilities, often used for semantic retrieval.
   - o **Vector Databases:** Solutions like FAISS, Pinecone, or Milvus are optimized for handling vectorized data from semantic search models.
2. **Installation and Configuration:**
   - o **Local Installation:**
     Download and install the chosen database on your local machine for development purposes. Follow the official installation guides for the respective database (e.g., MongoDB Community Edition or Elasticsearch OSS).
   - o **Cloud Deployment:**
     Many providers offer managed document store services (e.g., MongoDB Atlas, Amazon Elasticsearch Service) that simplify scaling, backups, and maintenance.
3. **Data Ingestion and Indexing:**
   - o **Data Preparation:**
     Preprocess and normalize documents to ensure consistency. This may involve cleaning text, removing stop words, or converting documents into a standard format (e.g., JSON).
   - o **Index Creation:**
     Create indices that allow efficient retrieval. For keyword-based search, define text indices; for semantic search, store vector embeddings alongside documents.
   - o **Data Upload:**
     Use batch insertion tools or APIs provided by the database to populate your document store. For instance, MongoDB's bulkWrite or Elasticsearch's Bulk API can be utilized for large datasets.

Managing Document Stores in Flowise AI

1. **Integration with Flowise AI:**
   - o **Connector Nodes:**
     Flowise AI includes dedicated nodes to interact with document stores. These nodes are configured to handle

operations like querying, inserting, updating, and deleting documents.

- o **Configuration:**
  In the node properties, specify connection parameters such as host, port, database name, and authentication credentials. Secure sensitive information using environment variables.

2. **Querying and Retrieval:**
   - o **Query Design:**
     Develop queries that leverage the strengths of your document store. For example, use full-text search for keyword queries or vector similarity queries for semantic search.
   - o **Re-ranking:**
     Optionally, use re-ranking strategies to prioritize retrieved documents that are most relevant to the input query, ensuring high-quality context is fed into the LLM.

3. **Maintenance and Updates:**
   - o **Index Refresh and Rebuild:**
     Periodically refresh indices to incorporate new documents and optimize query performance.
   - o **Data Archiving:**
     Implement strategies for archiving or purging outdated data to maintain store performance.
   - o **Monitoring and Scaling:**
     Use monitoring tools (e.g., MongoDB's Ops Manager, Elasticsearch's Kibana) to track query performance and system health. Scale resources as needed based on workload demands.

Best Practices

- **Consistent Data Schema:**
  Define and adhere to a clear data schema to ensure that documents are uniformly indexed and easily retrievable.
- **Efficient Indexing:**
  Optimize index settings based on your query patterns. For semantic searches, maintain a balance between index size and retrieval speed.
- **Security:**
  Secure your document store with appropriate authentication, encryption, and access controls. Regularly update your configurations to comply with security best practices.
- **Regular Backups:**
  Implement automated backups to safeguard your data. In cloud

environments, take advantage of managed backup services to ensure data integrity and availability.

Summary

Setting up and managing document stores is a foundational step in building effective RAG systems. By selecting the appropriate database, configuring it for efficient indexing and retrieval, and integrating it seamlessly with Flowise AI, you can provide the robust contextual data necessary for enhancing LLM outputs. Employing best practices in data management, security, and performance optimization ensures that your document store remains reliable, scalable, and effective in delivering high-quality context to your workflows.

5.2.1 Overview and Types (MongoDB, Elasticsearch, etc.)

Document stores serve as the backbone for Retrieval-Augmented Generation (RAG) systems by providing a structured repository for unstructured or semi-structured data. They enable efficient storage, indexing, and retrieval of documents, which are then used to enrich the context for LLM outputs. This section provides an overview of document stores and discusses various types commonly used in RAG systems.

Overview of Document Stores

- **Purpose:**
  Document stores are designed to handle large volumes of unstructured or semi-structured data such as text, JSON objects, images, and more. In the context of RAG systems, they allow you to store vast amounts of textual data—like articles, reports, and FAQs—which can be quickly searched and retrieved to provide context for language models.
- **Core Features:**
  - **Flexible Schema:** Unlike traditional relational databases, document stores use a flexible schema that allows for dynamic and heterogeneous data entries.
  - **Indexing Capabilities:** Efficient indexing supports both keyword-based and semantic search, ensuring fast retrieval of relevant documents.
  - **Scalability:** These systems are designed to scale horizontally, making them well-suited for handling large datasets and high query loads.

Types of Document Stores

- **MongoDB:**
  - **Description:** A popular NoSQL database known for its flexibility and ease of use with JSON-like documents.
  - **Strengths:**
    - Supports complex queries and aggregation pipelines.
    - Offers robust scalability and replication features.
    - Widely adopted with a large community and extensive documentation.
  - **Use Cases:** Ideal for applications that require dynamic schema design and real-time data updates.
- **Elasticsearch:**
  - **Description:** A powerful, distributed search and analytics engine built on top of Apache Lucene.
  - **Strengths:**
    - Optimized for full-text search and complex querying.
    - Provides advanced indexing and real-time analytics.
    - Supports both keyword-based and semantic search via its rich query DSL.
  - **Use Cases:** Best suited for scenarios where fast, accurate text search is critical—such as logging systems, e-commerce search, and data exploration.
- **Vector Databases (e.g., FAISS, Pinecone, Milvus):**
  - **Description:** Specialized databases designed for storing and querying high-dimensional vector embeddings.
  - **Strengths:**
    - Optimized for semantic search, leveraging vector similarity measures (e.g., cosine similarity) to find contextually relevant documents.
    - Efficient at handling large-scale embedding collections, which is essential for modern AI applications.
  - **Use Cases:** Particularly useful when integrating semantic search techniques with RAG systems, allowing you to retrieve documents based on the conceptual similarity of text.

Choosing the Right Document Store

- **Data Characteristics:**
  Consider the structure and volume of your data. MongoDB is

excellent for unstructured data with a flexible schema, while Elasticsearch is optimal for complex search and analytics.

- **Search Requirements:**
  If your application demands fast, sophisticated text search and analytics, Elasticsearch may be the better choice. For semantic search based on embeddings, vector databases like FAISS or Pinecone provide specialized capabilities.
- **Scalability Needs:**
  Assess your scalability requirements. All three options are designed to handle large datasets, but your choice may depend on the expected query load and the need for horizontal scaling.
- **Integration with RAG Systems:**
  Ensure that your chosen document store can be seamlessly integrated into your RAG workflow. This includes supporting efficient data ingestion, robust indexing, and rapid retrieval to provide the necessary context for the generative model.

Summary

Document stores are essential for enhancing RAG systems by providing a repository of contextual data that informs LLM outputs. Whether you choose MongoDB for its flexibility, Elasticsearch for its advanced search capabilities, or a vector database for semantic retrieval, each type offers distinct advantages tailored to different data and application needs. Understanding these options helps you select the most appropriate solution for your workflow, ensuring that your RAG system is both efficient and scalable.

5.3.2 Real-World Case Studies (Customer Support, Knowledge Bases)

Real-world case studies provide invaluable insights into how Retrieval-Augmented Generation (RAG) systems can be deployed effectively. Below are two examples that illustrate practical implementations in customer support and knowledge management.

Case Study 1: Enhanced Customer Support

Objective:
Automate and enhance customer support interactions by generating context-aware, precise responses to user queries.

Workflow Overview:

- **User Query Capture:**
  A customer submits a query via a chat interface, for example, "How do I reset my password?"
- **Context Retrieval:**
  A RAG node queries a knowledge base containing FAQs, support articles, and troubleshooting guides. Using semantic search, the retriever fetches the most relevant documents that describe the password reset process.
- **Response Generation:**
  The LLM node receives both the user query and the retrieved context. By integrating the information from support documents, the LLM generates a detailed, accurate response that explains the password reset process step-by-step.
- **Post-Processing and Delivery:**
  A processing node refines the response to ensure clarity and remove any extraneous information before the final answer is displayed to the customer.

Benefits:

- **Improved Accuracy:**
  The integration of real-time, context-specific information reduces the likelihood of generic or incorrect responses.
- **Reduced Support Load:**
  Automated, context-aware responses allow customer support teams to focus on more complex issues, improving overall efficiency.
- **Enhanced User Experience:**
  Quick and accurate responses contribute to higher customer satisfaction and engagement.

Case Study 2: Dynamic Knowledge Base Integration

Objective:
Facilitate rapid information retrieval and summarization from large knowledge bases for research or internal support, ensuring that users can quickly access relevant information.

Workflow Overview:

- **Document Ingestion:**
  A comprehensive knowledge base is maintained with documents such as technical manuals, policy documents, and research articles. These documents are indexed in a document store that supports both keyword and semantic search.
- **User Query and Retrieval:**
  A user submits a query, for example, "What are the latest updates to the company's data security policy?" The retrieval node searches the document store for the most relevant sections of the policy document using semantic similarity measures.
- **Summarization and Integration:**
  The retrieved content is passed to an LLM node which summarizes the key updates in a concise manner. In some implementations, a multi-step process is used where initial summaries are further refined through reprocessing.
- **Final Output:**
  The summarized information is presented to the user in a clear, digestible format, possibly accompanied by links to the full documents for further details.

Benefits:

- **Efficient Information Access:**
  Users can quickly obtain critical information without manually sifting through large volumes of text.
- **Consistency and Accuracy:**
  By dynamically retrieving and summarizing content, the system ensures that responses are based on the most current version of documents.
- **Adaptability:**
  As the knowledge base is updated, the RAG system automatically integrates new information, ensuring that users always receive up-to-date responses.

Summary

These case studies demonstrate the real-world impact of integrating RAG systems into customer support and knowledge management workflows. In customer support, RAG systems leverage contextual retrieval to generate accurate, actionable responses, thereby reducing workload and enhancing user satisfaction. In knowledge bases, dynamic retrieval and summarization empower users to access and understand vast amounts of information quickly and reliably. Together, these implementations highlight the versatility and effectiveness of RAG systems in transforming traditional information retrieval into intelligent, context-driven interactions.

5.4 Advanced Optimization Techniques for RAG Systems

Optimizing RAG systems is essential for maximizing the quality, efficiency, and responsiveness of your AI workflows. Advanced optimization techniques focus on enhancing both the retrieval and generation components, ensuring that the system delivers contextually accurate and timely outputs. Below are several strategies to optimize RAG systems:

1. Enhancing Retrieval Efficiency

- **Indexing Optimization:**
  - **Tailored Index Structures:**
    Use specialized indexing methods for your document store. For keyword searches, optimize text indices (e.g., using BM25 parameters in Elasticsearch) and for semantic searches, fine-tune vector indices (e.g., FAISS or Pinecone) to improve retrieval speed and relevance.
  - **Data Preprocessing:**
    Standardize and clean your documents before indexing. Normalizing text, removing stop words, and stemming can improve the efficiency of traditional keyword searches.
- **Hybrid Search and Re-Ranking:**
  - **Hybrid Retrieval Models:**
    Combine keyword-based and semantic search techniques to leverage the strengths of both. Initially retrieve a broad set of documents using keyword search, then refine the results with semantic re-ranking using vector similarity measures.
  - **Custom Re-Ranking Algorithms:**
    Implement neural re-ranking models that assess the contextual relevance of retrieved documents, adjusting the final ranking based on advanced similarity metrics or learned heuristics.
- **Query Expansion:**
  - Enhance search queries with synonyms and related terms using natural language processing (NLP) techniques. Query

expansion can capture additional relevant documents that might otherwise be missed by a strict keyword search.

2. Optimizing Generation Performance

- **Prompt Engineering:**
  - ○ **Context-Driven Prompts:**
    Craft prompts that effectively blend the user query with retrieved context. Experiment with different formats and hierarchies (e.g., separating the query from context using clear delimiters) to guide the generative model.
  - ○ **Dynamic Prompt Adjustments:**
    Utilize adaptive prompt strategies that modify the prompt based on real-time feedback or the characteristics of the retrieved documents.
- **Fine-Tuning Model Parameters:**
  - ○ **Temperature and Token Limits:**
    Optimize settings such as temperature and maximum tokens to balance creativity with precision. Lower temperatures often yield more deterministic outputs, while higher values increase variability.
  - ○ **Iterative Refinement:**
    Adopt multi-step generation processes where the initial output is refined through subsequent passes. This iterative approach can help to progressively align the generated text with the desired context.

3. Leveraging Caching and Parallelism

- **Caching Strategies:**
  - ○ **Intermediate Result Caching:**
    Cache frequently retrieved documents or intermediate summaries to reduce repeated computation and API calls. This is especially beneficial for high-frequency queries.
  - ○ **Result Reuse:**
    Store final outputs for common queries, so that similar requests can be answered immediately without re-executing the full workflow.
- **Parallel Processing:**
  - ○ **Concurrent Retrieval:**
    Distribute retrieval tasks across multiple nodes or threads to speed up the process of fetching documents.

- Asynchronous Generation:
  Implement asynchronous API calls for the LLM node,
  enabling the system to continue processing while waiting for
  responses, thereby reducing overall latency.

4. Continuous Monitoring and Iterative Improvement

- **Performance Metrics and Logging:**
  - **Real-Time Monitoring:**
    Use monitoring tools to track key performance indicators
    such as retrieval time, response time, and output quality.
    Analyze logs to identify bottlenecks and error patterns.
  - **Feedback Loops:**
    Incorporate user feedback and system performance metrics
    into an iterative refinement process. Regularly update your re-
    ranking models, prompt designs, and caching strategies based
    on observed performance.
- **Scalability and Resource Allocation:**
  - **Adaptive Scaling:**
    Utilize cloud-native tools like Kubernetes to automatically
    scale resources in response to workload changes. Horizontal
    scaling can improve throughput, while vertical scaling may be
    used to handle peak loads.
  - **Resource Management:**
    Monitor resource usage (CPU, memory, network) to ensure
    that no single component becomes a bottleneck. Optimize
    code and adjust configurations to achieve a balanced
    workload distribution.

Summary

Advanced optimization techniques for RAG systems involve a
comprehensive approach that spans efficient indexing and retrieval, strategic
prompt engineering, caching and parallelism, and continuous performance
monitoring. By combining these strategies, you can significantly improve the
accuracy, speed, and overall robustness of your RAG workflows. This
holistic optimization ensures that the generative model not only produces
high-quality, contextually relevant outputs but also operates efficiently in a
scalable, real-time environment.

Chapter 6: Designing and Orchestrating Agentic Workflows

6.1 Introduction to Agentic Workflows

Agentic workflows represent a paradigm shift in designing complex, autonomous AI systems. Rather than relying on a monolithic process where a single system handles every task, agentic workflows break down operations into multiple independent agents. Each agent is responsible for a specific task, operating autonomously while coordinating with others to achieve a common goal. This modular approach not only enhances scalability and efficiency but also improves fault tolerance and adaptability in dynamic environments.

Key Characteristics

- **Autonomy:**
  Each agent functions independently, executing its designated task based on predefined rules or dynamic inputs without requiring continuous oversight.
- **Modularity:**
  The workflow is composed of discrete, interchangeable agents. This modularity allows developers to easily add, remove, or update individual components without overhauling the entire system.
- **Coordination:**
  Although autonomous, agents communicate through well-defined protocols to share information and synchronize actions. This coordination is crucial for maintaining the integrity and coherence of the overall workflow.
- **Scalability:**
  Agentic workflows can be scaled horizontally by adding more agents to handle increased workload or more complex tasks. This flexibility makes them well-suited for large-scale, distributed systems.
- **Fault Tolerance:**
  The independent nature of agents ensures that if one agent fails, it can be isolated and replaced without causing a complete system breakdown. This resilience is vital in production environments where uptime is critical.

Benefits in Modern AI Applications

- **Improved Efficiency:**
  By delegating tasks to specialized agents, processes can run in parallel, reducing overall execution time and optimizing resource utilization.
- **Enhanced Flexibility:**
  Developers can tailor individual agents to specific functions, allowing for customization and fine-tuning according to the unique requirements of different applications.
- **Dynamic Adaptation:**
  Agentic workflows are particularly effective in environments where data and conditions change rapidly. Agents can adapt in real time, ensuring that the system remains responsive and accurate.

Use Cases

- **Data Processing Pipelines:**
  Each agent can handle a specific phase—data extraction, cleaning, transformation, and analysis—resulting in efficient, end-to-end processing.
- **Customer Support Systems:**
  Autonomous agents can manage various aspects of customer interactions, such as query classification, response generation, and follow-up actions, creating a robust multi-agent support system.
- **Automated Decision-Making:**
  In scenarios like financial analysis or supply chain management, different agents can independently evaluate data and collectively contribute to making informed decisions.

Summary

In summary, agentic workflows are a powerful approach for orchestrating complex AI systems. By dividing tasks among autonomous, modular agents, these workflows offer enhanced scalability, resilience, and efficiency. As you delve deeper into this chapter, you'll learn how to design and implement these workflows using Flowise AI, leveraging agent-based architectures to build robust and adaptive AI applications.

6.1.1 Defining Agentic Workflows and Their Benefits

Agentic workflows are an innovative approach in AI system design that divide complex tasks into discrete, autonomous units—known as agents—that work both independently and collaboratively. Instead of a single, monolithic process handling every step, agentic workflows delegate specific responsibilities to individual agents. Each agent is programmed to perform a well-defined function, making the overall system more flexible, scalable, and resilient.

Defining Agentic Workflows

- **Modular Structure:**
  In agentic workflows, each agent is a self-contained module tasked with executing a specific function within the larger process. These modules can be developed, deployed, and maintained independently, yet they are interconnected through clear communication channels that allow for coordinated operations.
- **Autonomous Operation:**
  Each agent operates independently, executing its assigned tasks based on internal logic or dynamic inputs. This autonomy reduces the need for centralized control and allows each component to react to changes in real time.
- **Coordinated Collaboration:**
  Although agents work independently, they also interact and exchange data to ensure that their individual outputs contribute effectively to the overall goal. This coordinated collaboration is achieved through defined protocols and data exchange mechanisms.

Benefits of Agentic Workflows

- **Enhanced Scalability:**
  Because agents are modular and operate in parallel, additional agents can be added to handle increased workload or more complex tasks without a complete system overhaul. This makes it easier to scale applications horizontally.
- **Improved Fault Tolerance:**
  The independence of each agent means that if one agent fails, it can be isolated or replaced without disrupting the entire workflow. This compartmentalization enhances system reliability and minimizes downtime.

- **Flexibility and Customization:**
  Agentic workflows allow developers to fine-tune individual agents for specific tasks. This flexibility means that workflows can be easily adapted or expanded as new requirements emerge, making the system more responsive to evolving business needs.
- **Efficiency Through Parallel Processing:**
  Agents can process different tasks concurrently, significantly reducing overall execution time compared to sequential processing. This parallelism leads to faster data processing and improved throughput in high-demand applications.
- **Simplified Maintenance and Updates:**
  Since agents operate as independent units, updating or modifying one agent does not necessitate changes to the entire system. This modularity simplifies maintenance, facilitates iterative improvements, and accelerates the development cycle.

Summary

Defining agentic workflows as modular, autonomous, and collaboratively orchestrated systems provides a powerful framework for tackling complex AI challenges. Their benefits—ranging from enhanced scalability and fault tolerance to improved efficiency and maintenance—make them an ideal solution for modern, dynamic applications. As you continue through this chapter, you will learn how to design, implement, and optimize these workflows using Flowise AI, leveraging the strengths of individual agents to build robust and adaptive AI systems.

6.1.2 Comparing Agentic and Traditional Workflows

Understanding the differences between agentic workflows and traditional, monolithic workflows is key to appreciating the advantages of a modular, agent-based design. Below is a detailed comparison that highlights their distinctive characteristics and benefits.

Structure and Modularity

- **Traditional Workflows:**
  Traditional workflows typically follow a sequential or centralized design. In these systems, a single monolithic process handles all tasks, which often leads to tightly coupled components.
  - **Pros:** Simplicity in design and straightforward execution for linear, less complex tasks.

- o **Cons:** Limited flexibility, as changes in one part of the workflow can impact the entire system.
- **Agentic Workflows:**
Agentic workflows decompose tasks into independent, autonomous agents, each responsible for a specific function. These agents operate modularly and communicate through well-defined interfaces.
  - o **Pros:** High modularity allows for easy updates, maintenance, and scalability. Individual agents can be developed, tested, and replaced without affecting the entire system.
  - o **Cons:** Requires robust communication protocols and coordination mechanisms, which may introduce complexity in system design.

Autonomy and Flexibility

- **Traditional Workflows:**
Components in traditional workflows are generally interdependent, meaning that the entire process may need to wait for a single component to complete its task before moving forward.
  - o **Impact:** Less resilient to disruptions; a failure in one component can halt the entire workflow.
- **Agentic Workflows:**
Each agent in an agentic workflow operates autonomously, making decisions based on local logic and input. This independence allows agents to work concurrently and adapt dynamically to changes.
  - o **Impact:** Enhanced fault tolerance; if one agent fails, the rest of the system can continue functioning, and the failed agent can be isolated or replaced without affecting overall operations.

Scalability and Performance

- **Traditional Workflows:**
Scaling traditional workflows often involves scaling the entire system as a whole, which can be inefficient and resource-intensive.
  - o **Challenges:** Sequential processing may lead to longer execution times and higher latency, especially as workload increases.
- **Agentic Workflows:**
The modular nature of agentic workflows enables horizontal scaling. Individual agents can be duplicated or distributed across multiple nodes to handle increased load.

o **Benefits:** Parallel processing reduces execution time and improves overall performance. This approach is particularly effective in handling complex or high-volume tasks.

Maintenance and Evolution

- **Traditional Workflows:**
  Due to their monolithic structure, traditional workflows can be challenging to maintain and evolve. Modifications often require extensive testing to ensure that changes do not disrupt the entire system.
  o **Impact:** Slower innovation and higher risk during updates.
- **Agentic Workflows:**
  The decoupled design of agentic workflows simplifies maintenance and iterative development. Each agent can be independently updated, refined, or replaced with minimal impact on the overall system.
  o **Impact:** Faster adaptation to new requirements, easier integration of new technologies, and reduced downtime during maintenance.

Use Cases and Application Domains

- **Traditional Workflows:**
  Best suited for simpler, linear tasks or when the complexity of interactions is minimal. They are often found in legacy systems where simplicity and stability are prioritized over flexibility.
- **Agentic Workflows:**
  Ideal for complex, dynamic environments where tasks are multifaceted and require parallel processing. They excel in applications such as data processing pipelines, autonomous systems, customer support platforms, and any scenario where scalability and resilience are critical.

Summary

While traditional workflows offer simplicity and ease of use for straightforward tasks, they often fall short in terms of flexibility, scalability, and resilience when faced with complex, dynamic environments. In contrast, agentic workflows provide a modular, autonomous approach that enhances fault tolerance, facilitates parallel processing, and simplifies maintenance.

This makes agentic workflows a powerful paradigm for modern AI applications that demand adaptability and robust performance.

6.2 Creating Autonomous Agents

Creating autonomous agents is a critical step in building agentic workflows. This process involves designing and developing individual modules that can operate independently to perform specific tasks within a larger system. Each autonomous agent is crafted to handle a distinct function, while also interacting with other agents to achieve a unified goal. Below are the key steps and considerations for creating effective autonomous agents.

1. Define the Agent's Role and Responsibilities

- **Task Specification:**
  Clearly outline the specific task that the agent will perform. For example, an agent may be responsible for data extraction, preprocessing, analysis, or decision-making.
- **Input and Output Requirements:**
  Determine what data the agent will receive (input) and what form its output should take. This helps in designing the interface between agents and ensuring seamless data flow across the workflow.
- **Operational Parameters:**
  Identify any parameters, thresholds, or business logic that will govern the agent's behavior. This may include conditions for triggering actions, error handling routines, and performance benchmarks.

2. Design the Agent Architecture

- **Modularity:**
  Structure the agent as a self-contained module with its own logic, configuration, and processing capabilities. Modular design makes it easier to test, maintain, and scale individual agents without impacting the entire system.
- **Inter-Agency Communication:**
  Define clear protocols for how the agent will communicate with other agents. This might involve using APIs, message queues, or shared data stores to exchange information reliably.
- **State Management:**
  Decide whether the agent will be stateless or maintain internal state. Stateless agents are easier to scale and recover, while stateful agents

might be necessary for tasks requiring continuity or historical context.

3. Develop and Implement the Agent

- **Programming Environment:**
  Choose a suitable programming language and framework based on the task. Python, for example, is widely used for data processing and AI-related tasks, while JavaScript or Node.js may be appropriate for real-time applications.
- **Core Functions and Methods:**
  Write the functions that define the agent's behavior. For example, if creating a data extraction agent, implement methods to fetch data from external sources, validate the data, and format it appropriately.
- **Error Handling and Resilience:**
  Incorporate robust error handling within the agent. Use try-except blocks (or equivalent constructs) to catch exceptions, log errors, and, if possible, retry operations. This ensures the agent remains resilient in the face of transient issues.
- **Example (Python Pseudocode):**

```python
Copy code
class DataExtractionAgent:
    def __init__(self, source_url):
        self.source_url = source_url

    def fetch_data(self):
        try:
            # Simulate data fetching from an API or database
            response = requests.get(self.source_url)
            response.raise_for_status()  # Check for HTTP errors
            return response.json()
        except Exception as e:
            # Log the error and implement fallback strategies
            print(f"Error fetching data: {e}")
            return None

    def process_data(self, data):
        # Implement data validation and transformation logic
        if data:
            # Transform or filter data as needed
```

```
            processed_data = [item for item in data if
self.validate(item)]
            return processed_data
        return []

    def validate(self, item):
        # Placeholder for validation logic
        return True

    def run(self):
        raw_data = self.fetch_data()
        return self.process_data(raw_data)

# Example usage:
agent =
DataExtractionAgent("https://api.example.com/data")
extracted_data = agent.run()
print("Extracted Data:", extracted_data)
```

4. Test and Optimize the Agent

- **Unit Testing:**
  Develop unit tests to validate each function within the agent. Testing individual components helps ensure that the agent performs as expected under different scenarios.
- **Performance Tuning:**
  Profile the agent to identify any bottlenecks or inefficient operations. Optimize code paths and, if necessary, refactor the design to improve performance.
- **Iterative Refinement:**
  Continuously gather feedback from testing and real-world usage. Use this feedback to iterate on the design, updating functionality, and improving error handling mechanisms.

5. Integrate the Agent into the Workflow

- **Connector Configuration:**
  Once the agent is developed and tested, integrate it into your agentic workflow using Flowise AI's visual workflow builder. Connect the agent's input and output nodes appropriately to ensure smooth data flow.
- **Inter-Agent Coordination:**
  Ensure that the agent can communicate and synchronize with other agents as needed. This might involve setting up messaging protocols or shared data repositories.

Summary

Creating autonomous agents involves a systematic approach that starts with defining clear roles and responsibilities, designing a modular architecture, and implementing robust, resilient code. By testing and optimizing each agent, and then integrating it into the broader workflow, you can build a highly efficient, scalable, and fault-tolerant system. This agent-based design empowers your AI workflows to handle complex tasks dynamically while remaining adaptable to evolving requirements.

6.2.1 Defining Agent Roles and Responsibilities

A crucial step in creating effective agentic workflows is clearly defining the roles and responsibilities of each autonomous agent. This step ensures that every agent has a well-understood function within the overall system, and that the agents work together seamlessly to achieve the desired outcome. Below are key considerations and strategies for defining agent roles and responsibilities:

Key Considerations

- **Task Specialization:**
  Determine the specific function each agent will perform within the workflow. This could range from data ingestion and preprocessing to analysis, decision-making, or output formatting. Clearly defined tasks help ensure that agents are focused and efficient in their operations.
- **Interface Definition:**
  Specify the inputs required and outputs produced by each agent. This ensures that data flows smoothly between agents, with clearly established protocols for communication and data exchange. Defining interfaces minimizes ambiguity and reduces the risk of errors during integration.
- **Operational Boundaries:**
  Clearly outline the limits of an agent's functionality. Defining what an agent is not responsible for can prevent overlaps and conflicts between different components, ensuring that each agent remains focused on its core tasks.
- **Autonomy and Interdependence:**
  Balance the need for individual autonomy with the necessity of collaboration. While each agent should be capable of functioning independently, it's important to define how agents interact, share

data, and support each other's operations to maintain overall system coherence.

Defining Roles and Responsibilities

- **Input Agent:**
  - **Role:** Collect data from external sources, user inputs, or sensors.
  - **Responsibilities:** Validate and normalize incoming data, and prepare it for further processing.
  - **Example:** A data ingestion agent that retrieves real-time market data and formats it for analysis.
- **Processing Agent:**
  - **Role:** Transform and analyze data to extract insights or prepare it for decision-making.
  - **Responsibilities:** Execute specific data transformations, apply filtering or computations, and handle error checking during processing.
  - **Example:** An agent that cleanses and aggregates raw data from various inputs to produce a unified dataset.
- **Decision-Making Agent:**
  - **Role:** Analyze processed data to make informed decisions or trigger actions.
  - **Responsibilities:** Apply business logic, machine learning models, or rule-based systems to generate actionable outputs.
  - **Example:** An agent that evaluates processed data to determine if a customer's issue requires escalation.
- **Output Agent:**
  - **Role:** Deliver the final results or responses to users, other systems, or databases.
  - **Responsibilities:** Format and transmit outputs, log critical information, and handle user notifications.
  - **Example:** An agent that presents a summarized report on a dashboard or sends notifications via email.
- **Coordination Agent (Optional):**
  - **Role:** Manage the interactions between multiple agents to ensure smooth workflow execution.
  - **Responsibilities:** Synchronize operations, manage dependencies, and orchestrate communication channels among agents.

- o **Example:** An agent that schedules tasks and monitors the status of individual agents, ensuring that delays or failures are quickly addressed.

Summary

Defining agent roles and responsibilities is fundamental to the success of agentic workflows. By clearly specifying what each agent is responsible for, from data ingestion to decision-making and output, you ensure that tasks are effectively distributed and executed in a coordinated manner. This structured approach not only enhances system efficiency and scalability but also simplifies troubleshooting and future enhancements, making your AI workflows more robust and adaptable to changing requirements.

6.2.2 Designing Communication and Data Sharing Channels

Effective communication and data sharing between autonomous agents are critical for ensuring a cohesive, well-coordinated agentic workflow. This section outlines strategies and best practices for establishing robust channels that allow agents to exchange information, synchronize actions, and collectively drive the workflow toward its overall objectives.

Key Principles

- **Clear Protocols:**
  Establish standardized communication protocols that define how messages, data, and signals are exchanged between agents. This minimizes misunderstandings and ensures that all agents interpret shared information consistently.
- **Decoupling and Modularity:**
  Design channels that allow agents to operate independently while still being able to share data when necessary. Decoupling the communication layer from the agents' core logic promotes modularity and simplifies maintenance.
- **Scalability:**
  Ensure that the communication framework can handle an increasing number of agents and higher volumes of data without becoming a bottleneck. Scalable communication channels support both real-time interactions and asynchronous data sharing.

Designing Communication Channels

- **Message Formats and Standards:**
  Define clear message formats (e.g., JSON, XML) that encapsulate all necessary information such as sender ID, timestamp, and data payload. Using standard formats simplifies integration and troubleshooting.
- **Communication Modes:**
  - **Synchronous Communication:**
    Use synchronous channels for tasks that require immediate responses and real-time coordination. This might be implemented via REST APIs or WebSocket connections.
  - **Asynchronous Communication:**
    For tasks that do not require instant responses, asynchronous methods such as message queues (e.g., RabbitMQ, Kafka) or publish-subscribe models can improve overall system efficiency and resilience.
- **Middleware Solutions:**
  Leverage middleware solutions or message brokers to facilitate reliable message delivery and buffering. This helps manage traffic spikes and ensures that messages are not lost if an agent is temporarily unavailable.

Data Sharing Strategies

- **Shared Data Repositories:**
  Establish a centralized or distributed data repository (such as a database or a shared cache) where agents can read and write information. This allows agents to access a common source of truth, ensuring consistency across the workflow.
- **Direct Peer-to-Peer Communication:**
  In scenarios where latency is critical, agents may communicate directly with each other using peer-to-peer protocols. This approach can reduce overhead but requires robust error handling to manage direct dependencies.
- **Data Versioning and Timestamping:**
  Implement data versioning and timestamping to track changes and ensure that agents are operating on the most recent and relevant information. This is especially important in dynamic environments where data evolves rapidly.

Best Practices

- **Error Handling and Acknowledgments:**
  Incorporate mechanisms for error detection, message acknowledgments, and retries to ensure reliable communication. This includes logging communication errors and defining fallback procedures when data exchange fails.
- **Security Measures:**
  Secure communication channels using encryption (e.g., TLS/SSL), authentication, and authorization protocols. Protect sensitive data by ensuring that only authorized agents can access or modify shared information.
- **Monitoring and Logging:**
  Use monitoring tools to track the performance and reliability of communication channels. Detailed logs help in diagnosing issues, analyzing communication patterns, and optimizing the data sharing process over time.

Summary

Designing effective communication and data sharing channels is fundamental for successful agentic workflows. By establishing clear protocols, choosing appropriate communication modes, and implementing robust data sharing strategies, you can ensure that autonomous agents collaborate seamlessly. These practices not only improve the efficiency and scalability of your system but also enhance its resilience and adaptability in dynamic environments.

6.3 Implementing Multi-Agent Systems

Multi-agent systems (MAS) are at the heart of agentic workflows, enabling complex tasks to be decomposed into smaller, specialized agents that work together to achieve a common objective. This section outlines the process of implementing multi-agent systems within Flowise AI, detailing design considerations, integration techniques, and best practices for building robust, scalable, and resilient systems.

Overview

- **Definition:**
  Multi-agent systems consist of multiple autonomous agents that

interact, collaborate, and sometimes compete to complete tasks. Each agent performs a specific function within the workflow, such as data extraction, processing, decision-making, or output generation.

- **Objective:**
  The goal is to leverage the collective strengths of individual agents to handle complex, dynamic tasks more efficiently than a monolithic system could.

Design Considerations

- **Modularity:**
  Each agent should be designed as a self-contained module with clearly defined inputs, outputs, and functionality. This modularity simplifies testing, maintenance, and future upgrades.
- **Inter-Agent Communication:**
  Establish robust communication channels (both synchronous and asynchronous) to ensure that agents can share data and coordinate actions effectively. Consider using message queues or shared data repositories to facilitate this interaction.
- **Scalability and Fault Tolerance:**
  Design the system so that agents can operate in parallel and can be scaled independently. If one agent fails, the system should have mechanisms in place to isolate the failure and continue functioning with minimal disruption.
- **Coordination and Control:**
  While agents operate autonomously, a higher-level orchestration or coordination layer (such as a coordination agent or workflow manager) may be necessary to manage task dependencies and ensure overall workflow coherence.

Step-by-Step Implementation

1. **Define Agent Roles:**
   - Clearly identify the specific tasks each agent will handle (e.g., data ingestion, preprocessing, decision-making, output formatting).
   - Document the expected inputs and outputs for each agent.
2. **Develop Individual Agents:**
   - Implement the core logic for each agent in a modular fashion using a programming language such as Python.
   - Ensure that each agent includes error handling, logging, and retry mechanisms to manage failures gracefully.

o For example, a data extraction agent might fetch data from an external API, validate the input, and format it for further processing.

3. **Establish Communication Protocols:**
   o Choose suitable communication channels (e.g., REST APIs, WebSockets, message queues) based on the required response times and data exchange volume.
   o Define message formats (e.g., JSON) that encapsulate essential information such as agent identifiers, timestamps, and payload data.

4. **Integrate Agents into the Workflow:**
   o Use Flowise AI's Visual Workflow Builder to arrange and connect individual agent nodes.
   o Ensure that the output from one agent feeds correctly into the input of the next, maintaining a seamless data flow throughout the workflow.

5. **Implement a Coordination Mechanism:**
   o Optionally, develop a coordination agent or controller that oversees the interactions between agents, schedules tasks, and monitors overall system health.
   o This layer can handle complex scenarios, such as managing dependencies between agents or triggering fallback procedures if an agent fails.

Integration with Flowise AI

- **Node Representation:**
  In Flowise AI, each autonomous agent is represented as a node within the visual workflow. These nodes encapsulate the agent's functionality and are connected to form a complete multi-agent system.
- **Configuration:**
  Configure each agent node via the Properties Panel to specify details such as data sources, processing parameters, and communication endpoints.
- **Monitoring and Logging:**
  Leverage Flowise AI's built-in logging and monitoring tools to track the performance and interactions of each agent. Real-time logs can help identify bottlenecks and provide insights for iterative improvements.

Testing and Optimization

- **Unit and Integration Testing:**
  Conduct thorough unit tests on individual agents to ensure they function as expected. Follow up with integration testing to verify that communication between agents is reliable and that the overall system achieves its intended outcomes.
- **Performance Profiling:**
  Monitor key metrics such as execution time, resource utilization, and throughput. Identify and optimize any performance bottlenecks, particularly in communication channels or data processing steps.
- **Iterative Refinement:**
  Use feedback from testing and real-world usage to continuously refine agent behaviors, improve coordination mechanisms, and adjust system parameters for optimal performance.

Summary

Implementing multi-agent systems involves designing and building autonomous, modular agents that collaborate to handle complex tasks within a coordinated workflow. By defining clear roles, establishing robust communication channels, integrating agents using Flowise AI's visual tools, and rigorously testing the system, you can create scalable, fault-tolerant workflows that efficiently address dynamic challenges. This multi-agent approach not only enhances system performance but also provides the flexibility needed to adapt to evolving requirements in modern AI applications.

6.3.1 Step-by-Step Design and Code Walkthroughs

In this section, we provide a detailed, step-by-step guide to designing and implementing a multi-agent system using Flowise AI. We'll outline the overall design process, and then dive into a code walkthrough that illustrates how individual agents can be developed, connected, and orchestrated to work collaboratively within a multi-agent workflow.

Step 1: Define the System Requirements

- **Identify Tasks:**
  Break down the overall task into specific subtasks that can be handled by separate agents. For example, consider a system that processes customer orders:
    o **Data Ingestion Agent:** Retrieves incoming order data.
    o **Validation Agent:** Checks data quality and order completeness.
    o **Processing Agent:** Calculates totals and applies discounts.
    o **Notification Agent:** Sends confirmation emails.
- **Define Inputs and Outputs:**
  Determine the expected inputs and outputs for each agent, ensuring that the output of one agent is formatted appropriately to serve as the input for the next.
- **Determine Communication Needs:**
  Decide on the communication method for passing data between agents (e.g., using message queues, REST API calls, or shared data repositories).

Step 2: Design the Agent Architecture

- **Modular Agent Classes:**
  Design each agent as a self-contained module or class with a clear interface. Each class should have methods for processing data, handling errors, and logging outputs.
- **Inter-Agent Communication:**
  Plan how agents will exchange messages. In our walkthrough, we'll assume a simplified direct method call to simulate communication in a controlled environment.
- **Coordination Layer:**
  Optionally design a controller or coordinator that sequences agent execution and handles exceptions.

Step 3: Code Walkthrough Example

Below is an example implementation in Python that simulates a multi-agent system for processing customer orders.

```python
Copy code
import time
import random

# Base class for agents to provide logging and error handling
class BaseAgent:
    def log(self, message):
        print(f"[{self.__class__.__name__}] {message}")

    def handle_error(self, error):
        self.log(f"Error: {error}")

# Agent 1: Data Ingestion Agent
class DataIngestionAgent(BaseAgent):
    def fetch_order_data(self):
        # Simulate data retrieval (e.g., from an API or
database)
        self.log("Fetching order data...")
        time.sleep(1)  # simulate network delay
        # Example order data
        orders = [
            {"order_id": 101, "items": ["apple", "banana"],
"total": 0},
            {"order_id": 102, "items": ["orange"], "total":
0}
        ]
        self.log("Order data fetched.")
        return orders

# Agent 2: Validation Agent
class ValidationAgent(BaseAgent):
    def validate_orders(self, orders):
        self.log("Validating order data...")
        valid_orders = []
        for order in orders:
            # Check if the order contains at least one item
            if order["items"]:
                valid_orders.append(order)
            else:
                self.handle_error(f"Order {order['order_id']}
has no items.")
        self.log(f"Validated {len(valid_orders)} orders.")
        return valid_orders
```

127

```python
# Agent 3: Processing Agent
class ProcessingAgent(BaseAgent):
    def process_orders(self, orders):
        self.log("Processing orders...")
        for order in orders:
            # Simulate processing: calculate total by a
random price per item
            order["total"] = sum(random.uniform(1.0, 5.0) for
_ in order["items"])
            self.log(f"Order {order['order_id']} processed
with total ${order['total']:.2f}.")
        return orders


# Agent 4: Notification Agent
class NotificationAgent(BaseAgent):
    def send_notifications(self, orders):
        self.log("Sending notifications for processed
orders...")
        for order in orders:
            # Simulate sending a notification
            self.log(f"Notification sent for Order
{order['order_id']} with total ${order['total']:.2f}.")
        self.log("All notifications sent.")
        return True


# Controller to orchestrate agent execution
class OrderProcessingController:
    def __init__(self):
        self.ingestion_agent = DataIngestionAgent()
        self.validation_agent = ValidationAgent()
        self.processing_agent = ProcessingAgent()
        self.notification_agent = NotificationAgent()

    def run_workflow(self):
        # Step 1: Ingest order data
        orders = self.ingestion_agent.fetch_order_data()

        # Step 2: Validate order data
        valid_orders =
self.validation_agent.validate_orders(orders)

        # Step 3: Process orders
        processed_orders =
self.processing_agent.process_orders(valid_orders)

        # Step 4: Send notifications
        notifications_sent =
self.notification_agent.send_notifications(processed_orders)

        return notifications_sent
```

```
# Example of executing the multi-agent workflow
if __name__ == "__main__":
    controller = OrderProcessingController()
    result = controller.run_workflow()
    if result:
        print("Multi-agent workflow executed successfully.")
    else:
        print("Workflow encountered errors.")
```

Explanation:

- **BaseAgent:**
  A simple base class providing logging and error handling functionality that other agents inherit from.
- **Individual Agents:**
  - **DataIngestionAgent:** Simulates fetching order data.
  - **ValidationAgent:** Checks orders to ensure they contain items.
  - **ProcessingAgent:** Processes orders by calculating a total using simulated pricing.
  - **NotificationAgent:** Simulates sending notifications for each processed order.
- **Controller:**
  The `OrderProcessingController` orchestrates the workflow, sequentially executing each agent and ensuring that data flows properly from one stage to the next.
- **Execution:**
  The `if __name__ == "__main__":` block runs the complete workflow and logs outputs for each step.

Step 4: Testing and Iterative Refinement

- **Unit Tests:**
  Develop unit tests for each agent to validate functionality in isolation.
- **Integration Tests:**
  Test the entire workflow using the controller to ensure agents interact as expected.
- **Performance Monitoring:**
  Log execution times and resource usage to identify and optimize any bottlenecks.

- **Feedback and Improvement:**
  Use real-world data and feedback to refine individual agents and improve inter-agent communication protocols.

Summary

This step-by-step design and code walkthrough demonstrates how to implement a multi-agent system using a modular architecture. By defining clear agent roles, establishing robust communication and data-sharing methods, and orchestrating the agents through a controller, you can build scalable, resilient workflows. This approach not only simplifies complex task management but also enables efficient debugging, testing, and iterative improvement, forming a solid foundation for advanced AI applications using Flowise AI.

6.3.2 Practical Use Cases and Interactive Examples

Practical use cases and interactive examples are invaluable for understanding how multi-agent systems can be applied to solve real-world problems. In this section, we explore various scenarios where multi-agent systems enhance workflow efficiency, followed by interactive examples that demonstrate the principles in action.

Use Cases

- **Data Processing Pipelines:**
  In complex data environments, multi-agent systems can decompose tasks such as data extraction, cleaning, transformation, and aggregation. For instance, one agent might extract raw data from multiple sources, another cleans and normalizes the data, while a third aggregates the results for analysis. This modular design enables parallel processing and faster turnaround times.
- **Autonomous Customer Support Systems:**
  Multi-agent systems can revolutionize customer support by assigning specific roles to different agents. One agent could handle query classification, another could retrieve relevant support articles (using RAG techniques), and a third could generate personalized responses. This division of labor enhances response accuracy and reduces workload on human support staff.

- **Intelligent Decision-Making in Finance:**
  In financial systems, separate agents can monitor market trends, analyze risk, and execute trading strategies in real time. Autonomous agents operating in parallel ensure rapid response to market fluctuations, improving decision-making efficiency and reducing the risk associated with manual intervention.
- **IoT and Smart City Management:**
  Smart city systems can use multi-agent workflows to manage various tasks such as traffic monitoring, energy distribution, and public safety. Each agent processes data from sensors, makes localized decisions, and communicates with central systems, allowing for adaptive and responsive city management.

Interactive Examples

- **Interactive Data Pipeline Simulation:**
  Imagine a visual simulation where you can drag and drop agents to build a data processing pipeline. An interactive tool could allow you to simulate real-time data flows—showing how one agent extracts data, another processes it, and a third aggregates the final results. Users can adjust parameters like processing speed or data volume and see the effect on overall pipeline performance.
- **Customer Support Chatbot Scenario:**
  An interactive demo might simulate a customer support session where a multi-agent system handles a query. One panel shows an agent classifying the query, another retrieves relevant FAQ content, and a third generates a customized response. Users can modify aspects such as query complexity or agent configurations to observe changes in response quality and latency.
- **Financial Market Simulation:**
  Another example could involve a simulated trading environment where agents monitor stock prices, analyze trends, and execute trades. An interactive dashboard would allow users to see how individual agent decisions contribute to overall trading performance, and how the system adapts to simulated market volatility.

Summary

By examining practical use cases—from data processing and customer support to financial systems and smart city management—and engaging with interactive examples, you gain a deeper understanding of how multi-agent systems work in real-world applications. These scenarios illustrate the modularity, scalability, and fault tolerance of agentic workflows, while interactive examples provide hands-on experience in designing, configuring, and optimizing multi-agent systems using Flowise AI. This comprehensive approach not only reinforces the theoretical concepts but also empowers you to apply them effectively in your projects.

6.4 Debugging and Optimizing Agentic Workflows

Debugging and optimizing agentic workflows are critical to maintaining robust, efficient, and scalable multi-agent systems. Given the complexity of coordinating multiple autonomous agents, effective troubleshooting and performance tuning can significantly enhance system reliability and responsiveness. This section outlines strategies, tools, and best practices for identifying issues and refining agentic workflows in Flowise AI.

Debugging Strategies

- **Granular Logging and Monitoring:**
  - **Centralized Logs:**
    Use Flowise AI's logging framework to capture detailed logs for each agent. Centralized logging allows you to correlate events across agents and identify where errors or performance bottlenecks occur.
  - **Real-Time Dashboards:**
    Monitor system metrics such as processing times, data throughput, and resource usage via real-time dashboards. These insights help pinpoint issues quickly.
- **Isolating Agents for Unit Testing:**
  - **Modular Testing:**
    Test individual agents in isolation using unit tests to verify that each component behaves as expected.
  - **Simulation Environments:**
    Run agents with simulated inputs to reproduce errors under controlled conditions, enabling focused debugging without the complexity of full workflow interactions.
- **Step-by-Step Workflow Execution:**
  - **Incremental Execution:**
    Execute the workflow in stages, verifying the output at each step. This incremental approach helps identify which specific stage is causing issues.

- o **Breakpoints and Debug Modes:**
  Utilize breakpoints or debug modes in your development environment to pause execution and inspect intermediate data and agent states.
- **Error Handling and Fallbacks:**
  - o **Graceful Degradation:**
    Implement error-handling mechanisms within each agent so that failures do not cascade through the system. Agents should provide fallback outputs or retry logic when encountering errors.
  - o **Alerting and Notifications:**
    Set up automated alerts for critical failures. Immediate notifications help reduce downtime by prompting swift intervention.

Optimization Techniques

- **Performance Profiling:**
  - o **Resource Usage Analysis:**
    Profile individual agents and the overall workflow to monitor CPU, memory, and network utilization. Identify inefficient code paths or communication delays.
  - o **Bottleneck Identification:**
    Use profiling tools to identify which agents or interactions are slowing down the workflow, then target these areas for optimization.
- **Parallel Processing and Load Balancing:**
  - o **Concurrency Optimization:**
    Ensure that agents operating in parallel are not competing for limited resources. Optimize the number of parallel processes based on your hardware capabilities.
  - o **Distributed Deployment:**
    Leverage cloud orchestration tools (e.g., Kubernetes) to distribute agents across multiple nodes, balancing the load to improve response times and scalability.
- **Iterative Refinement and Tuning:**
  - o **Parameter Adjustment:**
    Continuously fine-tune agent-specific parameters, such as batch sizes, timeout settings, and retry intervals. Small adjustments can lead to significant performance improvements.

- o **Feedback Loops:**
  Implement mechanisms to collect performance data and user feedback, then use this information to iteratively refine your workflow design and agent logic.
- **Caching and Preprocessing:**
  - o **Intermediate Caching:**
    Cache results of frequently executed tasks or intermediate outputs to avoid redundant processing.
  - o **Data Preprocessing:**
    Preprocess data at the input stage to reduce the computational load on downstream agents.

Summary

Debugging and optimizing agentic workflows require a systematic approach that combines granular monitoring, modular testing, and iterative refinement. By employing robust logging and real-time dashboards, isolating and testing individual agents, and fine-tuning resource usage and communication strategies, you can ensure that your multi-agent system operates efficiently and reliably. These best practices not only help resolve issues quickly but also contribute to a scalable and resilient workflow architecture within Flowise AI.

Part III: Advanced Customization, Integration, and Deployment

---

Chapter 7: Harnessing the Flowise API

The Flowise API serves as a powerful bridge between your custom AI workflows and external systems, enabling seamless integration, automation, and extension of Flowise AI's capabilities. In this chapter, we explore how to effectively harness the Flowise API for advanced customization and integration. You'll learn about the API architecture, how to authenticate and interact with API endpoints, and best practices for building robust integrations.

7.1 Overview of the Flowise API Architecture

The Flowise API is designed as a modular, extensible interface that connects the powerful capabilities of Flowise AI with external systems. Its architecture is built to facilitate seamless integration, automation, and real-time control of AI workflows.

Key Architectural Components

- **RESTful Endpoints:**
  Flowise API endpoints follow standard REST conventions, using HTTP methods (GET, POST, PUT, DELETE) to manage resources such as workflows, nodes, and execution logs. This consistency makes it easier to integrate with a variety of programming environments and third-party services.
- **Modularity and Extensibility:**
  The API is designed to be modular, enabling developers to interact with different components of Flowise AI independently. Whether you need to create a new workflow, modify node configurations, or retrieve performance metrics, each API endpoint is organized to target a specific aspect of the platform.
- **Authentication and Security:**
  Access to the API is secured via API keys or tokens, ensuring that only authorized users can manipulate workflows and retrieve data. All communications are conducted over HTTPS, adding an essential layer of security to data transmission.
- **Scalability and Performance:**
  Flowise API is built to support scalable deployments. It can handle high volumes of requests, making it suitable for both small-scale experiments and enterprise-level applications. The underlying

architecture is optimized for rapid response times, even as the complexity and number of workflows increase.

- **Integration Flexibility:**
Designed with interoperability in mind, the API allows seamless integration with various external systems—from customer relationship management (CRM) platforms and data warehouses to custom dashboards and IoT devices. This flexibility ensures that Flowise AI can be embedded into a wide range of operational environments.

How It Works

- **Resource-Oriented Design:**
Each resource (e.g., workflows, nodes, logs) is represented as a distinct entity within the API. This resource-oriented approach simplifies both the understanding and the utilization of the API, allowing developers to quickly pinpoint and manipulate specific elements of the system.
- **Uniform Interface:**
The API's uniform interface enables consistent methods of data exchange, ensuring that operations like creation, retrieval, updating, and deletion follow predictable patterns. This uniformity aids in rapid development and debugging.
- **Real-Time Data Interaction:**
With endpoints designed for both synchronous and asynchronous operations, the Flowise API supports real-time interactions. This allows developers to trigger workflows, fetch real-time status updates, and integrate monitoring systems directly into their applications.

Benefits for Developers

- **Ease of Use:**
The RESTful design and clear documentation make it straightforward for developers to get started, reducing the learning curve and speeding up the integration process.
- **Customization:**
The modular nature of the API means that developers can customize workflows to meet specific needs, extending functionality by connecting Flowise AI with other systems or embedding it within larger software ecosystems.

- **Reliability and Security:**
  Built with enterprise-grade security features and robust error handling, the Flowise API ensures that your integrations are both secure and reliable.

Summary

The Flowise API architecture is a cornerstone of the Flowise AI platform, offering a flexible, scalable, and secure interface for integrating and managing AI workflows. Its RESTful, resource-oriented design, combined with modularity and strong security measures, empowers developers to build custom solutions that seamlessly integrate Flowise AI into diverse operational environments. As you work through this chapter, you'll gain practical insights into how to leverage these API capabilities to automate processes, connect with external systems, and extend the functionality of your AI applications.

7.2 Authentication, Security, and Rate Limiting

Securing your interactions with the Flowise API is paramount to protecting sensitive data and ensuring reliable operations. This section covers the essential aspects of authentication, security measures, and rate limiting strategies, which help safeguard your API usage while maintaining optimal performance.

Authentication

- **API Keys and Tokens:**
  - **Usage:**
    The Flowise API utilizes API keys or bearer tokens to authenticate requests. Each request must include the appropriate authorization header to verify the caller's identity.
  - **Implementation:**
    Store your API keys securely (e.g., in environment variables or secure vaults) and ensure they are transmitted over HTTPS.
  - **Example:**

```python
Copy code
headers = {
    "Content-Type": "application/json",
    "Authorization": f"Bearer {api_key}"
```

}

- **Role-Based Access Control (RBAC):**
  - ○ Define roles with specific permissions for different users or services.
  - ○ RBAC ensures that each API client only has access to the endpoints and resources necessary for their function.

Security Measures

- **HTTPS and Encryption:**
  - ○ **Encryption:**
    All API communications should occur over HTTPS to encrypt data in transit, protecting it from interception or tampering.
  - ○ **Certificates:**
    Validate SSL/TLS certificates to ensure you're communicating with the authentic API server.
- **Input Validation and Sanitization:**
  - ○ Validate all incoming data to prevent injection attacks and other malicious inputs.
  - ○ Sanitize outputs to ensure that sensitive data is not inadvertently exposed.
- **Logging and Monitoring:**
  - ○ **Activity Logs:**
    Maintain comprehensive logs of API requests and responses. This helps in identifying unusual patterns that might indicate security breaches.
  - ○ **Alerts:**
    Set up automated alerts to detect and respond to potential security incidents promptly.
- **Regular Key Rotation:**
  - ○ Periodically rotate API keys and tokens to minimize the risk associated with compromised credentials.
  - ○ Implement mechanisms to revoke and replace keys without disrupting service.

Rate Limiting

- **Purpose:**
  Rate limiting protects the API from abuse and ensures fair usage

among all clients by controlling the number of requests a client can make within a specific time frame.

- **Implementation Strategies:**
  - **Fixed Window:**
    Allow a maximum number of requests in a defined time window (e.g., 1000 requests per hour).
  - **Sliding Window:**
    Use a dynamic window to smooth out request bursts, providing a more flexible limit while preventing spikes.
  - **Token Bucket:**
    Clients are allocated tokens that replenish over time; each API request consumes a token. This method accommodates short bursts of high activity while enforcing long-term limits.
- **Response Handling:**
  - When a rate limit is exceeded, the API should return a standard HTTP status code (typically 429 Too Many Requests) along with a message indicating when the limit will reset.
  - Clients should implement exponential backoff or retry strategies to handle rate-limited responses gracefully.

Best Practices

- **Secure Storage of Credentials:**
  Ensure that all API keys, tokens, and sensitive credentials are stored in secure, non-public environments.
- **Consistent Monitoring:**
  Use monitoring tools to track API usage, detect anomalies, and adjust rate limits if necessary.
- **Client-Side Enforcement:**
  Implement rate limiting on the client side to prevent accidental overuse and to adhere to server-imposed limits.
- **Documentation and Guidelines:**
  Keep detailed documentation of your authentication and rate limiting policies so that all developers and system integrators are aware of and adhere to the guidelines.

Summary

Effective authentication, robust security measures, and thoughtful rate limiting are fundamental to maintaining the integrity, reliability, and performance of your interactions with the Flowise API. By employing secure

API keys and tokens, using HTTPS for encryption, validating inputs, and implementing rate limiting strategies, you can protect your system from unauthorized access and ensure a smooth, fair usage experience. These practices not only safeguard your data but also enhance the overall resilience of your AI applications integrated via the Flowise API.

7.3 Integrating External Systems and Services

Integrating external systems and services with Flowise AI extends the platform's capabilities, enabling you to build comprehensive, end-to-end AI solutions. This integration allows Flowise AI to act as a central orchestrator that not only manages internal workflows but also interacts seamlessly with other platforms such as CRMs, data warehouses, IoT devices, and custom dashboards. Below are key strategies and examples for achieving effective integration.

Key Integration Strategies

- **API-Based Connectivity:**
  Leverage RESTful or GraphQL APIs provided by external systems. Flowise AI can make API calls to fetch data, trigger actions, or push updates, ensuring that your AI workflows are continuously synchronized with other platforms.
- **Webhook Integration:**
  Configure webhooks to allow external systems to trigger workflows in Flowise AI automatically. This is useful for real-time event-driven interactions, such as initiating a workflow when new customer data is added to a CRM.
- **Data Synchronization:**
  Implement mechanisms to synchronize data between Flowise AI and external databases or data warehouses. This may involve periodic data pulls using scheduled tasks or real-time streaming via message queues (e.g., Kafka, RabbitMQ).
- **Middleware and Message Brokers:**
  Use middleware or message brokers to facilitate robust communication between Flowise AI and external systems. These components can handle load balancing, buffering, and routing of messages, ensuring reliable data exchange even during high-demand periods.
- **Direct Database Connectivity:**
  In some cases, it may be necessary to connect directly to external

databases (e.g., SQL or NoSQL) to perform complex queries or update records. Flowise AI can include nodes designed to handle database operations, ensuring smooth data integration.

Implementation Examples

- **CRM Integration:**
  - **Scenario:** Automatically update customer records or trigger support workflows when new leads are generated.
  - **Approach:** Use Flowise AI nodes to call CRM APIs (such as Salesforce or HubSpot) to retrieve lead data. Additionally, configure webhook endpoints that notify Flowise AI when certain CRM events occur, thereby triggering an appropriate workflow (e.g., a follow-up email sequence).
- **Data Warehouse Synchronization:**
  - **Scenario:** Aggregate data from various sources to generate comprehensive analytics reports.
  - **Approach:** Use API connectors to pull data from cloud-based data warehouses (like Snowflake or BigQuery) and combine it with internal data. Nodes can be configured to process and transform this data before generating insights or dashboards.
- **IoT Device Integration:**
  - **Scenario:** Monitor and analyze sensor data in real time to drive automated responses in smart environments.
  - **Approach:** Connect Flowise AI to IoT platforms via MQTT or RESTful APIs. Use dedicated nodes to ingest data from IoT devices, process the information, and trigger actions (such as sending alerts or adjusting environmental controls).
- **Custom Dashboard Integration:**
  - **Scenario:** Visualize real-time performance metrics and workflow statuses on a custom-built dashboard.
  - **Approach:** Flowise AI can push data to external dashboard services (e.g., Grafana or Tableau) via API calls. Alternatively, you can build a custom web interface that fetches data from Flowise AI's API endpoints, providing up-to-date insights into workflow performance.

Best Practices

- **Secure Data Transmission:**
Always ensure that data exchanged between Flowise AI and external systems is transmitted over secure protocols (HTTPS, TLS). Use

142

proper authentication methods (API keys, OAuth tokens) to protect sensitive information.

- **Error Handling and Retry Logic:**
  Implement robust error handling within your integration nodes. Use retry mechanisms and fallback procedures to manage transient errors, ensuring that your workflows remain resilient even when external systems experience issues.
- **Scalability and Load Management:**
  Design your integrations to handle varying loads. Consider using asynchronous communication methods and message queues to prevent bottlenecks, and monitor system performance to adjust resources as needed.
- **Documentation and Version Control:**
  Maintain clear documentation for all integration points, including API endpoints, data formats, and authentication details. Use version control to manage updates to integration code and configurations.

Summary

Integrating external systems and services with Flowise AI significantly expands the platform's functionality, allowing you to create interconnected, intelligent ecosystems. By leveraging APIs, webhooks, data synchronization techniques, and middleware solutions, you can build workflows that interact seamlessly with CRM systems, data warehouses, IoT devices, and custom dashboards. Following best practices in security, error handling, and scalability ensures that these integrations are robust, reliable, and able to meet the demands of real-world applications.

7.3.1 API Endpoints and Custom Integrations

API endpoints serve as the primary interface for interacting with Flowise AI, enabling custom integrations that extend the platform's functionality. In this section, we explore how to work with these endpoints and build tailor-made integrations to connect Flowise AI with external systems.

API Endpoints

- **Resource-Oriented Design:**
  Flowise AI's API endpoints are designed around resources—such as workflows, nodes, and execution logs—allowing for straightforward CRUD (Create, Read, Update, Delete) operations. Each endpoint is

dedicated to managing a specific aspect of the platform, which simplifies development and integration tasks.

- **Standardized HTTP Methods:**
  The API adheres to RESTful principles, utilizing standard HTTP methods:
  - **GET:** Retrieve information about workflows, nodes, or system status.
  - **POST:** Create new resources or trigger workflows.
  - **PUT/PATCH:** Update existing configurations or settings.
  - **DELETE:** Remove resources when no longer needed.
- **Uniform Data Formats:**
  JSON is the primary data format for both requests and responses, ensuring consistency and ease of parsing across different programming environments.

Custom Integrations

- **Connecting External Systems:**
  Custom integrations allow you to extend Flowise AI by interfacing with external services such as CRMs, data warehouses, or IoT platforms. For instance, you can design nodes that fetch data from an external database or trigger a workflow based on events received via webhooks.
- **Tailored Business Logic:**
  With custom integrations, you can incorporate specialized business logic into your workflows. This might involve aggregating data from multiple sources, reformatting information, or applying domain-specific transformations before the data enters your AI pipeline.
- **Flexible Endpoints:**
  The API provides endpoints that facilitate the integration process:
  - **Workflow Management Endpoints:** Create, update, or delete workflows programmatically.
  - **Execution Endpoints:** Trigger workflow runs, monitor execution status, and retrieve logs.
  - **Configuration Endpoints:** Adjust node settings and system configurations dynamically to adapt to changing requirements.

Example: Custom Integration Workflow

Consider a scenario where you need to integrate Flowise AI with a customer relationship management (CRM) system. You could design a custom integration with the following steps:

1. **Data Ingestion:**
    Use a GET endpoint to fetch new customer data from the CRM.
2. **Trigger Workflow:**
    Once new data is available, a POST request to a workflow execution endpoint triggers a workflow that processes customer information.
3. **Update CRM:**
    After processing, use a PUT endpoint to update the customer record in the CRM with insights generated by Flowise AI.
4. **Logging and Monitoring:**
    Retrieve logs via a GET endpoint to monitor the integration process and ensure that data exchange was successful.

Best Practices

*   **Secure Integration:**
    Use HTTPS and robust authentication (API keys, OAuth tokens) to ensure that all data exchanges are secure and authorized.
*   **Error Handling:**
    Implement comprehensive error handling and logging to capture any issues during API interactions. This ensures that integration failures are promptly identified and addressed.
*   **Documentation and Versioning:**
    Maintain detailed documentation of your custom integrations, including endpoint usage, data schemas, and authentication details. Version control these integrations to manage updates and maintain consistency over time.
*   **Testing and Iteration:**
    Test your custom integrations in isolated environments before deploying them to production. Iteratively refine the endpoints and integration logic based on real-world feedback and performance metrics.

Summary

API endpoints in Flowise AI provide a flexible, resource-oriented interface for managing workflows, nodes, and system configurations. By leveraging these endpoints, you can build custom integrations that connect Flowise AI with external systems, incorporate tailored business logic, and automate complex processes. Following best practices in security, error handling, and documentation ensures that your integrations are robust, reliable, and scalable, enabling a seamless expansion of Flowise AI's capabilities to meet diverse application needs.

7.3.2 Example Projects and Code Samples

This section provides practical examples of how to interact with the Flowise API by presenting projects and code samples that demonstrate common integration scenarios. These examples illustrate how you can use the API to manage workflows, trigger executions, and retrieve status information. The code samples are written in Python using the `requests` library, but the concepts are applicable across different programming environments.

Example 1: Retrieving a List of Workflows

Scenario:
Fetch the list of all workflows currently configured in your Flowise AI instance.

Code Sample:

```python
python
Copy code
import requests

# Define the API endpoint and authentication
api_url = "https://api.flowiseai.com/v1/workflows"
api_key = "YOUR_API_KEY_HERE"
headers = {
    "Content-Type": "application/json",
    "Authorization": f"Bearer {api_key}"
}

# Make the GET request to retrieve workflows
response = requests.get(api_url, headers=headers)

if response.status_code == 200:
    workflows = response.json()
    print("Workflows:", workflows)
else:
    print("Error retrieving workflows:",
response.status_code, response.text)
```

Explanation:

- The code sets up the API URL and headers (with authentication).
- It performs a GET request to the `/workflows` endpoint.
- On success, it prints the retrieved workflows; otherwise, it displays an error message.

Example 2: Triggering a Workflow Execution

Scenario:
Programmatically trigger a workflow run, passing in input data to start the execution.

Code Sample:

```python
python
Copy code
import requests

# Define the API endpoint for triggering a workflow run
api_url = "https://api.flowiseai.com/v1/workflow/run"
api_key = "YOUR_API_KEY_HERE"
headers = {
    "Content-Type": "application/json",
    "Authorization": f"Bearer {api_key}"
}

# Define the payload with the workflow ID and input data
payload = {
    "workflow_id": "workflow_12345",
    "input_data": {
        "user_query": "How do I reset my password?"
    }
}

# Make the POST request to trigger the workflow
response = requests.post(api_url, json=payload,
headers=headers)

if response.status_code == 200:
    run_status = response.json()
    print("Workflow Triggered Successfully:", run_status)
else:
    print("Error triggering workflow:", response.status_code,
response.text)
```

Explanation:

- This script sends a POST request to the `/workflow/run` endpoint with a JSON payload containing the workflow ID and associated input data.
- The response confirms whether the workflow was successfully triggered, and any returned status information is printed.

Example 3: Updating a Node's Configuration

Scenario:
Update the configuration of a specific node within a workflow. This can be useful when you need to adjust parameters dynamically.

Code Sample:

```python
python
Copy code
import requests

# Define the API endpoint for updating node configuration
api_url = "https://api.flowiseai.com/v1/node/update"
api_key = "YOUR_API_KEY_HERE"
headers = {
    "Content-Type": "application/json",
    "Authorization": f"Bearer {api_key}"
}

# Define the payload with the node ID and new configuration
settings
payload = {
    "node_id": "node_67890",
    "config": {
        "parameter_1": "new_value",
        "parameter_2": 10
    }
}

# Make the PUT request to update the node configuration
response = requests.put(api_url, json=payload,
headers=headers)

if response.status_code == 200:
    update_status = response.json()
    print("Node Configuration Updated:", update_status)
```

```
else:
    print("Error updating node configuration:",
response.status_code, response.text)
```

Explanation:

- This example demonstrates how to update a node's configuration using a PUT request.
- It sends the node ID and a configuration dictionary containing updated parameters.
- The API returns a status message confirming whether the update was successful.

Example 4: Retrieving Execution Logs

Scenario:
Fetch the logs for a specific workflow execution to monitor performance or troubleshoot issues.

Code Sample:

```python
python
Copy code
import requests

# Define the API endpoint for retrieving workflow logs
api_url = "https://api.flowiseai.com/v1/workflow/logs"
api_key = "YOUR_API_KEY_HERE"
headers = {
    "Content-Type": "application/json",
    "Authorization": f"Bearer {api_key}"
}

# Specify the workflow execution ID as a query parameter
params = {
    "execution_id": "exec_abc123"
}

# Make the GET request to retrieve the logs
response = requests.get(api_url, headers=headers,
params=params)

if response.status_code == 200:
    logs = response.json()
```

```
    print("Execution Logs:", logs)
else:
    print("Error retrieving logs:", response.status_code,
response.text)
```

Explanation:

- The script retrieves logs for a particular workflow execution by sending a GET request with an `execution_id` query parameter.
- Successful retrieval results in printing the log data; errors are appropriately handled.

Summary

These example projects and code samples illustrate how to leverage the Flowise API to integrate and manage your AI workflows. Whether you're retrieving workflow lists, triggering executions, updating configurations, or monitoring logs, these examples provide a practical foundation for building custom integrations. By following these examples and adapting them to your specific use cases, you can extend Flowise AI's functionality and seamlessly connect it with other systems and services in your technology stack.

Chapter 8: Advanced Customizations and Extensions

Advanced customizations and extensions empower you to tailor Flowise AI to meet specific, often complex, requirements that go beyond the default capabilities. This chapter explores techniques for developing custom nodes, integrating external libraries and third-party services, and extending the platform through plugins and performance enhancements. These advanced modifications enable you to build bespoke workflows, optimize system performance, and adapt Flowise AI to diverse operational environments.

8.1 Developing Custom Plugins and Extensions

Developing custom plugins and extensions is a powerful way to enhance Flowise AI's capabilities without altering its core codebase. This plugin architecture allows you to add new functionalities, integrate specialized external services, or tailor existing behaviors to meet unique project requirements. Here's how to approach creating custom plugins and extensions for Flowise AI:

Understanding the Plugin Architecture

- **Modularity:**
  Plugins are modular components that can be added or removed independently. This design ensures that custom extensions can be developed and maintained without affecting the stability of the core system.
- **Interfacing with Core Components:**
  Plugins interact with Flowise AI via clearly defined APIs and interfaces. This means your custom plugin must adhere to these protocols to communicate effectively with the system.
- **Seamless Integration:**
  Once developed, plugins are integrated into the Flowise AI ecosystem, typically appearing alongside built-in nodes in the Node Library. This seamless integration makes it easy to incorporate custom functionality into your workflows.

Steps to Develop a Custom Plugin

1. **Identify the Need:**
    Determine the specific functionality or integration that is not provided by the built-in nodes. This could range from connecting to an external data source, implementing a new data transformation logic, or adding custom visualization features.
2. **Design the Plugin:**
    - **Define Interfaces:**
      Specify what inputs the plugin will require and what outputs it will produce. Clearly document the expected data format, configuration options, and any dependencies.
    - **Outline Functionality:**
      Plan the internal logic of the plugin. Decide if it will operate as a standalone node or as an enhancer that modifies the behavior of existing nodes.
3. **Implement the Plugin:**
    - **Coding:**
      Develop the plugin using a supported programming language (often Python for Flowise AI). Inherit from the appropriate base classes provided by Flowise AI to ensure compatibility.
    - **Example Skeleton:**

```python
Copy code
from flowise.plugins import BasePlugin

class CustomTransformationPlugin(BasePlugin):
    def __init__(self,
name="CustomTransformation"):
        super().__init__(name)
        # Initialize any plugin-specific settings

    def process(self, input_data, config):
        """
        Apply custom transformation logic to the
input data.

        Args:
            input_data (dict): Data from the
previous node.
            config (dict): Custom configuration
parameters.

        Returns:
            dict: Transformed output data.
```

```
        """
        # Example: Transform text data by
appending a custom suffix
        try:
            transformed_data = {}
            for key, value in input_data.items():
                if isinstance(value, str):
                    transformed_data[key] =
f"{value} - transformed"
                else:
                    transformed_data[key] = value
            return transformed_data
        except Exception as e:
            self.log_error(f"Transformation
failed: {e}")
            return input_data  # Fallback to
original data

    def log_error(self, message):
        # Simple error logging mechanism
        print(f"[{self.name} ERROR]: {message}")

# Registration (this may vary depending on your
setup)
def register_plugin():
    # Flowise AI may offer a plugin registration
function
    from flowise.plugins import register
    register(CustomTransformationPlugin)
```

4. **Test Your Plugin:**
   o **Unit Testing:**
     Write unit tests to ensure your plugin functions correctly with different types of input data.
   o **Integration Testing:**
     Incorporate your plugin into a sample workflow in Flowise AI to validate its interaction with other nodes.
   o **Performance Monitoring:**
     Ensure that the plugin does not introduce significant latency or resource overhead.
5. **Documentation and Deployment:**
   o **Documentation:**
     Document the plugin's purpose, configuration parameters, and usage examples thoroughly. This helps future maintenance and enables other developers to use and extend your work.

o **Deployment:**
Once tested, deploy the plugin into your Flowise AI environment, ensuring that it appears in the Node Library for easy access.

Best Practices for Custom Plugin Development

- **Keep It Modular:**
Design plugins to be self-contained and focused on a single responsibility. This simplifies debugging and allows you to reuse plugins across multiple workflows.
- **Error Handling:**
Implement robust error handling within your plugins. Gracefully manage exceptions to prevent them from disrupting the entire workflow.
- **Optimize Performance:**
Profile and optimize your plugin code to ensure it runs efficiently, especially if it will be used in high-throughput or real-time scenarios.
- **Version Control:**
Use version control systems to manage your plugin code, facilitating collaboration and tracking changes over time.
- **Community Engagement:**
Consider sharing your plugins with the Flowise AI community. Collaborative feedback can help improve functionality and broaden the impact of your custom extensions.

Summary

Developing custom plugins and extensions allows you to tailor Flowise AI to your unique requirements by adding new functionalities or integrating external services seamlessly. By following a structured approach—defining clear interfaces, implementing robust code, thoroughly testing, and documenting your work—you can create powerful plugins that enhance your workflows while maintaining system stability and performance. This flexibility not only expands the capabilities of Flowise AI but also empowers you to build innovative, custom solutions that meet diverse application needs.

8.3 Performance Optimization and Scalability

Performance optimization and scalability are critical considerations when extending and customizing Flowise AI for advanced applications. As your workflows become more complex and handle increasing volumes of data, ensuring efficient execution and the ability to scale dynamically is essential. This section explores various strategies and best practices for optimizing performance and achieving scalability in your customizations and integrations.

Key Areas for Performance Optimization

- **Code Profiling and Benchmarking:**
  Regularly profile your custom nodes and plugins to identify bottlenecks. Use profiling tools to measure CPU, memory usage, and execution times. Benchmark different approaches to determine the most efficient implementation for your tasks.
- **Efficient Data Handling:**
  Optimize data ingestion and transformation processes by minimizing unnecessary computations. Utilize vectorized operations, efficient data structures, and batch processing techniques where applicable to reduce overhead.
- **Caching Mechanisms:**
  Implement caching at strategic points in your workflow. Cache frequently accessed data or intermediate results to avoid redundant processing. This is particularly useful in scenarios where external API calls or complex computations are involved.
- **Asynchronous and Parallel Processing:**
  Leverage asynchronous programming models to allow non-blocking operations, especially for I/O-bound tasks such as network requests. Design custom nodes to support parallel execution, distributing workloads across multiple cores or even multiple machines to enhance throughput.

Strategies for Scalability

- **Modular Architecture:**
  Ensure your customizations are designed as modular components. Modular design not only improves maintainability but also facilitates horizontal scaling, allowing you to add more instances of specific nodes or plugins as demand increases.

- **Distributed Processing:**
  Use containerization and orchestration tools like Docker and Kubernetes to deploy your workflows in distributed environments. This allows you to scale resources dynamically based on workload, ensuring high availability and responsiveness even under heavy loads.
- **Load Balancing:**
  Integrate load balancing mechanisms to distribute incoming tasks evenly across multiple instances of your workflows. This prevents any single node from becoming a performance bottleneck and helps maintain consistent response times.
- **Resource Management:**
  Monitor and adjust resource allocation based on performance metrics. Utilize tools for real-time monitoring of CPU, memory, and network usage, and implement auto-scaling policies that adjust resources in response to fluctuations in demand.

Best Practices

- **Iterative Optimization:**
  Adopt an iterative approach to performance tuning. Continuously monitor performance, gather feedback, and refine your implementation. Small, incremental improvements can lead to significant overall enhancements.
- **Comprehensive Testing:**
  Rigorously test your optimizations in environments that simulate real-world loads. Use stress tests and load tests to ensure that your system remains robust and responsive under high-demand conditions.
- **Documentation and Metrics:**
  Document performance benchmarks and optimization efforts. Establish key performance indicators (KPIs) to measure the impact of changes and ensure that any adjustments align with your scalability goals.
- **Community Collaboration:**
  Engage with the Flowise AI community to share insights, tools, and techniques for performance optimization. Collaborative efforts can help identify best practices and innovative approaches to scaling complex workflows.

Summary

Performance optimization and scalability are essential for maintaining robust, efficient, and responsive AI workflows as your applications grow in complexity. By focusing on efficient code, effective caching, asynchronous processing, and leveraging distributed systems, you can significantly enhance both the performance and scalability of your customizations in Flowise AI. These strategies not only ensure that your workflows can handle increased loads but also contribute to a more resilient and adaptable system capable of meeting the demands of modern AI applications.

8.3.1 Profiling, Benchmarking, and Optimization Techniques

To ensure that your customizations and integrations in Flowise AI perform at their best, it's essential to identify bottlenecks and optimize resource usage. Profiling, benchmarking, and targeted optimization techniques are key to achieving high performance and scalability in your workflows. This section outlines practical strategies and tools for measuring and improving the efficiency of your system.

Profiling Techniques

- **Code Profiling:**
  Use profiling tools to analyze the runtime behavior of your code. Profilers such as Python's `cProfile` or `line_profiler` can help you understand which parts of your code consume the most CPU time.
  - **Example (cProfile):**

    ```python
    Copy code
    import cProfile

    def run_workflow():
        # Your workflow execution code here
        pass

    cProfile.run('run_workflow()')
    ```

  - **Insight:** This will help pinpoint slow functions or loops that may need optimization.
- **Memory Profiling:**
  Monitoring memory usage is crucial, especially for data-intensive

operations. Tools like `memory_profiler` provide line-by-line memory consumption details.

- o **Example:**

```python
Copy code
from memory_profiler import profile

@profile
def process_data(data):
    # Your data processing logic here
    processed = [d * 2 for d in data]
    return processed

process_data(range(10000))
```

- o **Insight:** Identify memory leaks or inefficient data structures that could be replaced with more efficient alternatives.

Benchmarking Techniques

- **Execution Time Measurement:**
  Benchmark key functions and workflow segments to measure execution time. Python's `time` module or more sophisticated libraries like `timeit` can be used.
  - o **Example (timeit):**

```python
Copy code
import timeit

execution_time = timeit.timeit("run_workflow()",
setup="from __main__ import run_workflow",
number=10)
print("Average execution time:", execution_time /
10)
```

  - o **Insight:** Determine which parts of your workflow require optimization for better overall performance.
- **Load Testing:**
  Simulate high workloads to assess how your system scales under stress. Tools like Apache JMeter or custom scripts can help evaluate performance under varying loads.
  - o **Insight:** Identify performance bottlenecks when scaling and ensure the system remains responsive.

Optimization Techniques

- **Algorithmic Improvements:**
  Review and refine your algorithms to reduce computational complexity. For instance, replace inefficient loops with vectorized operations using libraries like NumPy or Pandas when processing large datasets.
- **Caching:**
  Implement caching for repeated or resource-intensive operations. Caching intermediate results or frequently accessed data minimizes redundant computations.
  - **Example:** Use Python's `functools.lru_cache` to cache function results:

    ```python
    Copy code
    from functools import lru_cache

    @lru_cache(maxsize=128)
    def compute_expensive_operation(param):
        # Simulate a costly computation
        return param ** 2

    print(compute_expensive_operation(10))
    ```

  - **Insight:** This can significantly reduce execution time for repetitive tasks.
- **Parallel and Asynchronous Processing:**
  Utilize parallel processing to distribute workload across multiple cores or machines. Libraries like `multiprocessing` or asynchronous frameworks like `asyncio` can improve responsiveness.
  - **Example (multiprocessing):**

    ```python
    Copy code
    from multiprocessing import Pool

    def process_item(item):
        # Process a single data item
        return item * 2

    if __name__ == "__main__":
        with Pool(4) as pool:
            results = pool.map(process_item,
    range(1000))
        print(results)
    ```

- o **Insight:** Parallelizing independent tasks can reduce total execution time dramatically.
- **Asynchronous I/O:**
  For I/O-bound operations (e.g., API calls, file access), asynchronous programming helps avoid blocking the execution thread.
  - o **Example (asyncio):**

```python
Copy code
import asyncio
import aiohttp

async def fetch_data(session, url):
    async with session.get(url) as response:
        return await response.text()

async def main():
    async with aiohttp.ClientSession() as session:
        data = await fetch_data(session,
"https://api.example.com/data")
        print(data)

asyncio.run(main())
```

  - o **Insight:** Asynchronous operations can enhance the efficiency of workflows involving network or disk I/O.

Summary

By leveraging profiling and benchmarking tools, you can gain deep insights into the performance characteristics of your customizations in Flowise AI. Applying optimization techniques—ranging from algorithmic improvements and caching to parallel processing and asynchronous I/O—ensures that your workflows are both efficient and scalable. Continuous monitoring and iterative refinement of these strategies are key to maintaining robust, high-performance AI systems in dynamic production environments.

8.3.2 Best Practices for Extending Flowise AI

When extending Flowise AI through customizations, plugins, and integrations, it's essential to adhere to best practices that ensure your extensions are robust, maintainable, and scalable. The following guidelines provide a framework for successfully extending Flowise AI:

- **Modular Design:**
  Develop extensions as self-contained, modular components. This approach facilitates easier testing, maintenance, and reuse across multiple workflows without affecting core functionality.
- **Comprehensive Documentation:**
  Document every aspect of your extension, including its purpose, configuration options, expected inputs/outputs, and any external dependencies. Clear documentation is crucial for maintenance, collaboration, and future enhancements.
- **Robust Error Handling:**
  Implement thorough error handling and logging within your extensions. Gracefully manage exceptions and provide fallback mechanisms so that failures in one component do not disrupt the entire workflow.
- **Performance Optimization:**
  Profile your custom code to identify bottlenecks and optimize resource usage. Use caching where applicable, and consider asynchronous processing or parallel execution to enhance performance in resource-intensive tasks.
- **Security Considerations:**
  Ensure that your extensions adhere to security best practices. This includes secure storage of credentials, data validation, and sanitization to prevent vulnerabilities. Use HTTPS and proper authentication mechanisms when integrating with external services.
- **Scalability and Resource Management:**
  Design your extensions to support horizontal scaling. Ensure that they can be distributed across multiple nodes or containers, and use load balancing and resource monitoring to manage workload efficiently.
- **Iterative Testing and Feedback:**
  Conduct unit tests for individual modules and integration tests for the complete workflow. Collect performance metrics and user feedback, and iterate on your design to address issues and improve functionality over time.
- **Community Collaboration:**
  Engage with the Flowise AI community to share your extensions and gather insights. Contributing to open-source repositories and participating in forums can provide valuable feedback and drive continuous improvement.
- **Version Control:**
  Use version control systems (e.g., Git) to track changes in your

extension code. This enables easier collaboration, rollback of changes when necessary, and a clear history of updates.

By following these best practices, you can develop extensions that not only enhance Flowise AI's capabilities but also remain robust, secure, and adaptable as your needs evolve. These guidelines form the foundation for building a reliable ecosystem around your AI workflows, ensuring that your customizations integrate seamlessly and perform optimally in diverse production environments.

Chapter 9: Configuration, Deployment, and DevOps

Efficient configuration, deployment, and DevOps practices are critical for transitioning your Flowise AI workflows from development to production. This chapter focuses on strategies and best practices to configure the system for various environments, deploy it reliably, and manage ongoing operations through robust DevOps methodologies.

Configuration Management

- **Centralized Configuration:**
    - **Configuration Files:**
      Store system-wide settings (e.g., environment variables, API endpoints, and authentication keys) in centralized configuration files or services.
    - **Environment-Specific Configurations:**
      Create separate configuration profiles for development, testing, staging, and production environments. This ensures that each environment has the appropriate settings without manual intervention.
- **Dynamic Reconfiguration:**
    - Use tools that allow dynamic updates to configurations without restarting the system. This capability is crucial for rapidly adapting to new requirements or scaling changes.
- **Version Control:**
    - Maintain all configuration files under version control. This practice enables you to track changes, roll back to previous configurations, and audit modifications over time.

Deployment Strategies

- **Local vs. Cloud Deployments:**
    - **Local Deployment:**
      Suitable for development, testing, and small-scale use. Allows for direct control over the environment and easy debugging.

163

- o **Cloud Deployment:**
  Ideal for scalable, production-grade systems. Cloud platforms such as AWS, Azure, or Google Cloud offer managed services, high availability, and elastic scaling.
- **Containerization:**
  - o **Docker:**
    Package your Flowise AI application along with its dependencies into Docker containers. Containers ensure consistency across development, testing, and production environments.
  - o **Benefits:**
    Simplifies deployment, enhances portability, and improves scalability by isolating the application from the underlying system.
- **Orchestration:**
  - o **Kubernetes:**
    Use Kubernetes or other container orchestration tools to manage multiple container instances, load balancing, scaling, and automated rollouts/rollbacks.
  - o **Best Practices:**
    Implement health checks, auto-scaling, and resource quotas to maintain high performance and availability.
- **CI/CD Pipelines:**
  - o **Continuous Integration:**
    Automate the testing and integration of code changes using CI tools like Jenkins, GitLab CI/CD, or GitHub Actions. This helps ensure that new changes do not break the existing system.
  - o **Continuous Deployment:**
    Automate deployment processes so that successful builds are automatically deployed to staging or production environments. Use blue-green or canary deployment strategies to minimize downtime and risk.
  - o **Testing Automation:**
    Integrate unit tests, integration tests, and end-to-end tests into your pipeline to catch issues early in the development cycle.

DevOps Best Practices

- **Infrastructure as Code (IaC):**

- Use tools like Terraform, AWS CloudFormation, or Ansible to manage and provision infrastructure. IaC enables consistent, repeatable deployments and simplifies scaling.
- **Monitoring and Logging:**
  - Implement comprehensive monitoring using tools like Prometheus, Grafana, or ELK stack (Elasticsearch, Logstash, Kibana).
  - Set up centralized logging and alerting to detect issues quickly and maintain operational visibility.
- **Security and Compliance:**
  - Enforce security best practices in your deployment pipelines, including vulnerability scanning, automated security audits, and compliance checks.
  - Ensure data encryption both in transit and at rest, and use role-based access control (RBAC) to manage permissions.
- **Backup and Recovery:**
  - Regularly back up critical data and configurations.
  - Develop and test disaster recovery plans to ensure business continuity in the event of failures.
- **Documentation and Training:**
  - Maintain thorough documentation of deployment processes, system architecture, and operational procedures.
  - Provide training for team members to ensure that they understand and can effectively manage the deployment environment.

Summary

Chapter 9 covers the essential aspects of configuring, deploying, and managing Flowise AI in production environments. By leveraging best practices such as centralized configuration management, containerization with Docker, orchestration using Kubernetes, and robust CI/CD pipelines, you can ensure that your AI workflows are deployed reliably, scaled efficiently, and maintained with minimal downtime. Embracing DevOps methodologies, including infrastructure as code, comprehensive monitoring, and proactive security measures, not only optimizes performance but also enhances the overall resilience of your system in a dynamic production landscape.

9.1 Deployment Strategies

Deploying Flowise AI effectively is crucial for ensuring that your AI workflows perform reliably and can scale to meet increasing demands. This section outlines various deployment strategies that cater to different needs— from local development environments to large-scale, cloud-based production systems.

Local Deployment

- **Purpose:**
  Ideal for development, testing, and small-scale deployments, local installation offers full control over your environment and simplifies debugging.
- **Advantages:**
  o Direct access to the system for rapid prototyping.
  o Simplified troubleshooting and iterative development.
  o Minimal external dependencies.
- **Considerations:**
  o Limited scalability and potential resource constraints.
  o Not typically recommended for high-availability production systems.

Cloud Deployment

- **Purpose:**
  Cloud deployment is designed for production environments where scalability, reliability, and global accessibility are paramount.
- **Platforms:**
  o **AWS, Azure, Google Cloud:**
  These cloud providers offer managed services that can host Flowise AI, providing built-in scalability, high availability, and robust security.
  o **Managed Services:**
  Use services like AWS Elastic Container Service (ECS) or Azure Kubernetes Service (AKS) to simplify orchestration and scaling.
- **Advantages:**
  o Elastic scaling to handle fluctuating workloads.
  o Enhanced reliability with distributed architecture and failover mechanisms.

- o Global reach with low-latency access to users worldwide.
- **Considerations:**
  - o Costs may scale with usage.
  - o Requires careful configuration of security, networking, and monitoring settings.

Containerization

- **Docker:**
  - o Package Flowise AI and its dependencies into a Docker container for consistent deployment across different environments.
  - o **Advantages:**
    - Portability: Containers run consistently on any platform that supports Docker.
    - Isolation: Ensures that dependencies and configurations do not conflict with other applications.
    - Simplifies deployment and scaling.
- **Best Practices:**
  - o Keep container images lean by removing unnecessary files and dependencies.
  - o Use environment variables and configuration files to manage runtime settings.

Orchestration

- **Kubernetes:**
  - o Use Kubernetes to manage, scale, and deploy Docker containers in a distributed environment.
  - o **Advantages:**
    - Automated scaling and load balancing.
    - Self-healing mechanisms (e.g., automatic restarts and rollbacks).
    - Simplifies management of large-scale deployments.
- **Key Considerations:**
  - o Design robust health checks to monitor container status.
  - o Configure resource limits and auto-scaling policies to optimize performance.

CI/CD Pipelines

- **Continuous Integration:**
  - Automate the process of testing and integrating code changes using tools like GitHub Actions, Jenkins, or GitLab CI/CD.
- **Continuous Deployment:**
  - Set up pipelines that automatically deploy successful builds to your testing or production environments.
  - **Strategies:**
    - **Blue-Green Deployment:** Maintain two identical production environments to minimize downtime during updates.
    - **Canary Deployment:** Gradually roll out updates to a small subset of users before full-scale deployment.

Summary

Choosing the right deployment strategy for Flowise AI depends on your specific requirements—whether you're in the development phase or scaling a production system. Local deployments provide an accessible environment for development and testing, while cloud deployments offer scalability, reliability, and global reach. Containerization with Docker ensures consistency and portability, and orchestration tools like Kubernetes help manage large-scale, distributed environments efficiently. Finally, integrating CI/CD pipelines ensures that updates are deployed smoothly and reliably, maintaining system performance and minimizing downtime.

9.1.1 On-Premise vs. Cloud Deployments

Choosing between on-premise and cloud deployments for Flowise AI is a critical decision that depends on your organization's specific needs, budget, and operational requirements. Each deployment model offers distinct advantages and challenges, and understanding these differences can help you select the best approach for your AI workflows.

On-Premise Deployments

- **Definition:**
  On-premise deployments involve hosting Flowise AI on your organization's own hardware and data centers, where you have full control over the infrastructure.
- **Advantages:**

- o **Control and Customization:**
  Complete control over hardware, security configurations, and software customizations.
- o **Data Security and Compliance:**
  Sensitive data remains within your own premises, which can be essential for organizations with strict regulatory or compliance requirements.
- o **Predictable Costs:**
  Upfront capital expenditures and predictable operational costs once infrastructure is in place.
- **Challenges:**
  - o **Scalability Limitations:**
    Scaling hardware to accommodate increased workloads can be time-consuming and expensive.
  - o **Maintenance Overhead:**
    Requires dedicated IT resources for hardware maintenance, updates, and security patches.
  - o **Initial Investment:**
    High upfront costs for infrastructure procurement and setup.

Cloud Deployments

- **Definition:**
  Cloud deployments leverage third-party cloud service providers (e.g., AWS, Azure, Google Cloud) to host Flowise AI. These platforms offer managed services that abstract away much of the underlying infrastructure management.
- **Advantages:**
  - o **Scalability:**
    Easily scale resources up or down based on demand with minimal manual intervention.
  - o **Flexibility and Agility:**
    Rapid deployment and access to a broad range of integrated services (e.g., managed Kubernetes, serverless computing).
  - o **Reduced Maintenance:**
    Cloud providers handle infrastructure maintenance, security updates, and backup processes.
  - o **Global Reach:**
    Deploy applications across multiple regions to reduce latency and improve user experience.
- **Challenges:**

- Operational Costs:
  Ongoing operational expenses can be unpredictable,
  particularly with high usage or dynamic workloads.
- Data Security Concerns:
  Although cloud providers offer robust security measures,
  some organizations may have concerns about data sovereignty
  and compliance.
- Vendor Lock-In:
  Relying on specific cloud services may limit flexibility in
  switching providers or integrating with legacy systems.

Considerations for Choosing the Right Model

- **Workload and Scalability Needs:**
  Evaluate whether your application demands rapid scaling and high
  availability (favoring cloud) or if predictable, stable workloads are
  best served on-premise.
- **Budget and Cost Structure:**
  Consider the trade-offs between upfront capital investment versus
  ongoing operational expenses.
- **Data Sensitivity and Compliance:**
  Determine the level of control required over data storage and
  processing, particularly in regulated industries.
- **Resource and IT Expertise:**
  Assess whether your organization has the in-house expertise and
  resources to manage on-premise infrastructure, or if leveraging
  managed cloud services would be more efficient.

Summary

On-premise deployments offer enhanced control, customization, and security
by allowing organizations to manage their own infrastructure. In contrast,
cloud deployments provide superior scalability, flexibility, and reduced
maintenance overhead through managed services. The decision between on-
premise and cloud deployments for Flowise AI should be based on a
thorough evaluation of workload requirements, budget considerations, data
security needs, and available IT resources. By aligning your deployment
strategy with your organizational priorities, you can optimize the
performance and cost-efficiency of your AI workflows.

9.2 CI/CD and Automated Testing for AI Workflows

Integrating Continuous Integration (CI) and Continuous Deployment (CD) practices into your Flowise AI projects ensures that updates are consistently tested and deployed, reducing downtime and minimizing the risk of introducing errors into production. Automated testing further guarantees that workflows behave as expected, even as code changes and new features are added. This section outlines strategies, tools, and best practices for implementing CI/CD and automated testing in your AI workflows.

Continuous Integration (CI)

- **Automated Testing Pipelines:**
  Establish a CI pipeline that automatically runs a suite of tests (unit, integration, and end-to-end tests) whenever changes are pushed to your repository. This helps catch issues early in the development cycle.
- **Code Quality Checks:**
  Integrate static code analysis and linting tools (such as pylint or flake8 for Python) into the CI process. This ensures that code adheres to established standards and is free of common errors before merging changes.
- **Version Control Integration:**
  Use version control systems like Git, and integrate CI tools (e.g., GitHub Actions, Jenkins, or GitLab CI) to trigger automated builds and tests on every commit or pull request.

Continuous Deployment (CD)

- **Automated Deployment Pipelines:**
  Once the CI pipeline passes all tests, automatically deploy changes to staging or production environments using CD tools. This minimizes manual intervention and speeds up the release cycle.
- **Deployment Strategies:**
  - **Blue-Green Deployment:** Maintain two identical environments, switching traffic between them to ensure a smooth transition during updates.
  - **Canary Deployment:** Gradually roll out new changes to a small percentage of users before full-scale deployment, allowing for monitoring and quick rollback if issues are detected.

- **Rollback Mechanisms:**
  Implement automated rollback strategies so that if new changes cause issues, the system can revert to a previous stable state without significant downtime.

Automated Testing for AI Workflows

- **Unit Testing:**
  Develop unit tests for individual components such as custom nodes, plugins, and API integrations. This ensures that each part of your workflow functions correctly in isolation.
- **Integration Testing:**
  Test the interaction between different nodes in a workflow. Integration tests help confirm that data flows correctly between agents and that combined functionalities meet expected outcomes.
- **End-to-End Testing:**
  Simulate real-world usage scenarios to validate the entire workflow, from data ingestion to final output. Automated end-to-end tests can detect issues that might not be apparent during isolated testing.
- **Test Coverage and Metrics:**
  Monitor test coverage to ensure that most of your codebase is tested. Tools like Coverage.py can help identify untested areas that could lead to potential bugs.

Best Practices

- **Incremental Testing:**
  Adopt an incremental testing approach where new code is immediately covered by tests. This fosters a culture of quality and reduces the risk of introducing regressions.
- **Automated Feedback Loops:**
  Set up notifications and dashboards to receive immediate feedback on test results and deployment status. This helps teams quickly identify and address issues.
- **Parallel Execution:**
  Use parallel test execution to reduce the time required for testing, especially when dealing with large codebases or complex workflows.
- **Environment Consistency:**
  Ensure that the testing environment closely mirrors production. Containerization and infrastructure as code (IaC) can help replicate production settings, minimizing discrepancies.

Summary

Implementing CI/CD and automated testing for AI workflows in Flowise AI significantly enhances development speed, code quality, and system reliability. Automated CI pipelines ensure that all changes are rigorously tested before deployment, while CD practices streamline the rollout of updates. By integrating comprehensive unit, integration, and end-to-end tests—and adopting strategies such as blue-green or canary deployments—you create a robust framework that minimizes downtime, detects issues early, and maintains high-quality AI workflows in production.

9.3 Monitoring, Logging, and Troubleshooting

Ensuring that your Flowise AI deployments run smoothly in production requires robust monitoring, comprehensive logging, and effective troubleshooting strategies. This section discusses methods and tools to maintain operational visibility, detect issues early, and quickly resolve problems to minimize downtime.

Monitoring

- **Real-Time Performance Metrics:**
  Utilize monitoring tools (e.g., Prometheus, Grafana, or cloud provider-specific tools) to track key metrics such as CPU, memory, disk usage, and network throughput. Monitoring dashboards provide a live view of system health and can alert you to anomalies.
- **Application Health Checks:**
  Configure liveness and readiness probes within your deployment (especially when using orchestration tools like Kubernetes) to ensure that containers and nodes are functioning correctly. These probes help automatically restart or reschedule failed services.
- **Workflow and Node Monitoring:**
  Leverage Flowise AI's built-in monitoring capabilities to track workflow execution times, success/failure rates, and other performance indicators. Detailed metrics help identify bottlenecks or underperforming nodes.

Logging

- **Centralized Logging:**
  Implement a centralized logging system (such as ELK Stack, Fluentd,

or a cloud-based logging service) to aggregate logs from all components of your system. Centralized logs simplify the process of searching, filtering, and analyzing events across your entire environment.

- **Detailed Log Levels:**
  Use log levels (DEBUG, INFO, WARNING, ERROR, CRITICAL) appropriately to capture both routine operations and exceptional events. This granularity helps in distinguishing between normal behavior and potential issues that need immediate attention.
- **Structured Logging:**
  Format logs in a structured format (e.g., JSON) to facilitate automated parsing and analysis. Structured logs can be integrated with monitoring systems to trigger alerts based on specific patterns or error rates.

Troubleshooting

- **Automated Alerts and Notifications:**
  Set up automated alerts based on predefined thresholds for key performance metrics and log patterns. Alerts can be sent via email, SMS, or integrated with collaboration tools like Slack to ensure that your team is promptly informed of issues.
- **Root Cause Analysis:**
  When an issue is detected, use logs and monitoring data to perform a root cause analysis. Correlate events across different layers (application, container, infrastructure) to pinpoint where the problem originated.
- **Iterative Debugging:**
  Use techniques such as isolating components, testing in staging environments, and employing breakpoints or debug modes to isolate and resolve issues. Iterative debugging helps to incrementally narrow down the root cause without disrupting the entire system.
- **Documentation of Incidents:**
  Maintain an incident log that documents issues, their resolution, and any changes made to prevent recurrence. This historical data can help in identifying recurring issues and in planning system improvements.

Summary

By implementing robust monitoring, centralized and structured logging, and effective troubleshooting processes, you ensure that your Flowise AI deployments remain reliable and responsive. Continuous monitoring provides real-time visibility into system health, while comprehensive logging captures the detailed data needed for root cause analysis. Automated alerts and iterative debugging techniques enable your team to quickly identify and resolve issues, ensuring that your AI workflows operate smoothly and efficiently in production environments.

9.3.1 Best Practices for Production Environments

Ensuring that your Flowise AI workflows perform reliably in production requires adherence to best practices that enhance stability, security, and scalability. The following guidelines are essential for maintaining a robust production environment:

- **Robust Monitoring and Alerting:**
  - Implement real-time monitoring of system metrics (CPU, memory, network usage) and workflow performance using tools like Prometheus and Grafana.
  - Set up automated alerts for abnormal behavior or resource exhaustion to enable prompt response.
- **Centralized and Structured Logging:**
  - Aggregate logs from all components using centralized logging systems (e.g., ELK Stack, Fluentd) to streamline troubleshooting and analysis.
  - Use structured logging formats (such as JSON) to facilitate automated parsing and correlation of log data.
- **Health Checks and Self-Healing:**
  - Configure liveness and readiness probes (especially in Kubernetes environments) to detect and automatically recover from service failures.
  - Ensure that your system is designed to isolate and restart failing components without affecting overall workflow execution.
- **Security and Access Control:**
  - Secure API communications with HTTPS and enforce strict authentication and authorization mechanisms (e.g., API keys, RBAC).
  - Regularly update security patches, and employ vulnerability scanning to protect against emerging threats.
- **Scalability and Load Balancing:**
  - Design your infrastructure for horizontal scalability using container orchestration tools like Kubernetes.

- Implement load balancing strategies to distribute traffic evenly across instances and prevent any single component from becoming a bottleneck.
- **Disaster Recovery and Backups:**
  - Establish a comprehensive backup strategy for critical data and configurations, and test recovery procedures regularly to ensure business continuity.
  - Plan for redundancy with failover systems and multi-region deployments where appropriate.
- **Performance Optimization:**
  - Continuously profile and benchmark your workflows to identify and resolve performance bottlenecks.
  - Optimize resource allocation and consider implementing caching mechanisms to reduce latency in high-demand scenarios.
- **Documentation and Change Management:**
  - Maintain detailed documentation of your production environment, configuration settings, and deployment procedures.
  - Use version control and change management processes to track modifications and ensure that any changes can be rolled back if needed.
- **Regular Auditing and Compliance:**
  - Conduct periodic audits of your system's security, performance, and compliance with industry standards.
  - Keep abreast of regulatory requirements and adjust your environment accordingly to ensure ongoing compliance.

By following these best practices, you create a production environment that is resilient, secure, and capable of scaling with the demands of modern AI applications. These measures not only help minimize downtime and disruptions but also support continuous improvement and reliable performance for your Flowise AI workflows.

9.3.2 Tools and Techniques for Ongoing Maintenance

Ensuring the long-term reliability and performance of your Flowise AI deployments in production requires a proactive maintenance strategy. This involves employing a suite of tools and techniques that allow you to continuously monitor, update, and optimize your system. Below are some of the key tools and techniques recommended for ongoing maintenance:

Monitoring and Logging Tools

- **Prometheus and Grafana:**
  Utilize Prometheus to collect real-time metrics from your infrastructure, workflows, and containers. Grafana can then visualize these metrics, providing dashboards that highlight key performance indicators and help identify potential issues before they escalate.
- **ELK Stack (Elasticsearch, Logstash, Kibana):**
  Implement the ELK stack for centralized, structured logging. Elasticsearch stores log data, Logstash processes and enriches logs, and Kibana provides intuitive visualizations to analyze trends and troubleshoot errors.
- **Cloud Provider Monitoring:**
  Leverage built-in monitoring services offered by cloud providers (e.g., AWS CloudWatch, Azure Monitor, Google Cloud Monitoring) to track resource utilization and set up alerts for critical events.

Automated Maintenance Techniques

- **Scheduled Backups and Snapshots:**
  Set up automated backups of critical data, configurations, and application state. Regular snapshots ensure that you can quickly recover from unexpected failures or data corruption.
- **Auto-Scaling and Load Balancing:**
  Use container orchestration tools like Kubernetes to automatically scale your deployments based on current demand. Load balancing helps distribute traffic evenly, preventing resource exhaustion on any single instance.
- **Continuous Integration and Deployment (CI/CD):**
  Maintain your deployment pipeline with automated testing and integration. CI/CD tools (e.g., Jenkins, GitLab CI/CD, GitHub Actions) help ensure that updates and patches are deployed smoothly, with minimal downtime and regression risk.

Performance and Security Maintenance

- **Regular Performance Profiling:**
  Continuously profile your workflows to detect bottlenecks. Use tools like cProfile, memory_profiler, or cloud-based performance analysis services to optimize resource utilization and reduce latency.

- **Security Audits and Vulnerability Scanning:**
  Implement regular security audits using tools like OWASP ZAP or Nessus. Automated vulnerability scanning ensures that your system remains secure against emerging threats.
- **Configuration Management and Version Control:**
  Employ configuration management tools (e.g., Ansible, Terraform) to keep your infrastructure consistent and reproducible. Version control your configuration files and codebases to track changes and facilitate quick rollbacks when necessary.

Best Practices for Ongoing Maintenance

- **Establish a Maintenance Schedule:**
  Plan regular maintenance windows for software updates, system backups, and performance reviews. This proactive approach minimizes the risk of unexpected outages.
- **Implement Automated Alerts and Notifications:**
  Configure your monitoring tools to send alerts via email, SMS, or messaging platforms like Slack. Quick notifications enable your team to address issues before they impact users.
- **Documentation and Incident Logs:**
  Keep thorough documentation of your system architecture, configuration settings, and maintenance procedures. Maintain an incident log to track issues, resolutions, and lessons learned, which can guide future improvements.
- **Iterative Feedback and Continuous Improvement:**
  Use data from monitoring and user feedback to continuously refine your workflows. Regularly revisit your performance metrics and update configurations to adapt to changing demands.

Summary

Ongoing maintenance of Flowise AI in production is a multifaceted process that relies on robust monitoring, automated maintenance tools, regular performance and security audits, and thorough documentation. By employing tools like Prometheus, Grafana, the ELK stack, and cloud-native monitoring services, and by integrating CI/CD pipelines, auto-scaling, and configuration management practices, you can ensure that your AI workflows remain resilient, secure, and optimized for performance. This proactive approach to maintenance not only minimizes downtime but also supports the continuous evolution and scalability of your system in dynamic production environments.

Part IV: Operational Excellence and Future Directions

Chapter 10: Best Practices for Operational Excellence

Achieving operational excellence is key to ensuring that your Flowise AI workflows not only function reliably but also adapt efficiently to evolving demands. This chapter consolidates best practices that span workflow optimization, monitoring, security, and continuous improvement. By embracing these guidelines, you can create a production environment that is robust, scalable, and resilient, ensuring your AI systems deliver high performance and meet business objectives consistently.

10.1 Workflow Optimization and Efficiency

Achieving operational excellence in AI workflows hinges on continuously optimizing and refining your processes to deliver faster, more accurate, and resource-efficient outcomes. In this section, we explore best practices for optimizing workflows in Flowise AI, ensuring that each process runs at peak efficiency while maintaining scalability and reliability.

Key Strategies for Workflow Optimization

- **Identify and Eliminate Bottlenecks:**
  - **Performance Profiling:**
    Use profiling tools to analyze the execution of your workflows and identify slow-running nodes or inefficient data processing steps.
  - **Resource Analysis:**
    Monitor CPU, memory, and I/O usage to pinpoint resource-intensive operations and optimize them accordingly.
- **Streamline Data Flow:**
  - **Data Preprocessing:**
    Clean and preprocess data as early as possible to reduce the computational load on downstream nodes.
  - **Efficient Data Routing:**
    Design workflows to minimize unnecessary data transfers or redundant processing steps, ensuring that data flows smoothly and efficiently between nodes.
- **Optimize Node Configuration:**
  - **Parameter Tuning:**
    Experiment with different configuration settings (e.g., batch

sizes, timeout values, and processing intervals) to find the optimal balance between performance and resource utilization.

- ○ **Dynamic Reconfiguration:**
  Leverage tools that support dynamic updates to node configurations without requiring system downtime, allowing for rapid adaptation to changing workloads.

Techniques for Enhancing Efficiency

- **Parallel Processing:**
  - ○ **Concurrent Execution:**
    Enable parallel processing where possible by running independent nodes or tasks concurrently, reducing overall execution time.
  - ○ **Asynchronous Operations:**
    For I/O-bound tasks, such as API calls or file access, adopt asynchronous programming models to prevent blocking and improve responsiveness.
- **Caching and Reuse:**
  - ○ **Result Caching:**
    Cache frequently computed results or retrieved data to avoid redundant computations and minimize latency.
  - ○ **Shared Resource Pools:**
    Utilize shared caches or resource pools to manage data that is accessed by multiple nodes, enhancing efficiency and reducing load.
- **Algorithmic Improvements:**
  - ○ **Efficient Algorithms:**
    Review and refine the algorithms used in your processing nodes. Replace inefficient loops or recursive functions with optimized, vectorized operations using libraries like NumPy or Pandas.
  - ○ **Load Balancing:**
    Distribute computationally intensive tasks across multiple nodes or cores to prevent any single component from becoming a performance bottleneck.

Monitoring and Iterative Refinement

- **Real-Time Monitoring:**
  Deploy monitoring tools to capture real-time metrics on workflow

performance, such as execution time, error rates, and resource utilization. Tools like Prometheus and Grafana can provide dashboards to visualize these metrics.

- **Feedback Loops:**
  Implement continuous feedback mechanisms to gather insights from performance monitoring and user feedback. Use this information to iteratively refine workflows, adjust configurations, and upgrade processes for sustained efficiency.
- **Automated Testing:**
  Integrate performance benchmarks into your automated testing pipeline. Regular load testing and stress testing help ensure that workflows maintain efficiency under varying conditions.

Best Practices for Maintaining Efficiency

- **Documentation and Change Management:**
  Document optimization strategies, configuration changes, and performance improvements. Keeping a detailed log of adjustments helps in troubleshooting and ensures consistency over time.
- **Collaboration and Community Engagement:**
  Engage with the Flowise AI community to share best practices, exchange optimization tips, and learn from real-world experiences. Collaborative feedback can be invaluable in identifying novel efficiency enhancements.
- **Regular Reviews and Updates:**
  Periodically review your workflows and update them to incorporate new technologies, methodologies, or improvements. This proactive approach ensures that your system remains agile and continues to operate at optimal performance.

Summary

Optimizing workflows for operational excellence in Flowise AI involves a combination of targeted performance improvements, efficient data handling, and continuous monitoring. By identifying bottlenecks, leveraging parallel processing, implementing caching strategies, and embracing iterative refinement, you can significantly enhance workflow efficiency. These best practices ensure that your AI workflows are not only fast and scalable but also robust and resilient, capable of meeting the evolving demands of production environments.

10.2 Comprehensive Monitoring Strategies

Comprehensive monitoring is essential for ensuring the smooth operation and resilience of your Flowise AI workflows. By tracking key performance indicators and system metrics, you can detect issues early, respond promptly to anomalies, and continuously optimize your environment. The following strategies outline a robust monitoring approach:

1. System and Infrastructure Monitoring

- **Real-Time Metrics Collection:**
  Use tools like Prometheus to gather metrics such as CPU usage, memory consumption, disk I/O, and network traffic across all components of your deployment. These metrics help you understand resource utilization and identify potential performance bottlenecks.
- **Health Checks:**
  Implement liveness and readiness probes (especially in Kubernetes environments) to continuously assess the health of your containers and services. This proactive approach ensures that any failing components are automatically restarted or rescheduled.
- **Auto-Scaling and Load Balancing:**
  Integrate monitoring with auto-scaling policies that adjust resources in response to real-time metrics. Load balancing further distributes the workload evenly, ensuring that no single component is overwhelmed.

2. Application and Workflow Monitoring

- **Workflow Execution Metrics:**
  Monitor the execution times, success/failure rates, and throughput of individual workflows. Tools like Grafana can visualize these metrics, allowing you to track the efficiency of each node or process within your workflow.
- **Custom Dashboards:**
  Create tailored dashboards that consolidate critical data points. These dashboards should provide an overview of workflow status, error rates, and performance trends to help quickly identify and resolve issues.
- **Alerting Mechanisms:**
  Configure automated alerts that trigger when key performance thresholds are breached. Alerts can be delivered via email, SMS, or

integrated messaging platforms (e.g., Slack), enabling immediate action when issues occur.

3. Centralized Logging

- **Structured Logging:**
  Utilize structured logging formats (such as JSON) to ensure that log data from various components is consistent and easily searchable. This approach allows for more efficient analysis and correlation of events across the system.
- **Centralized Log Management:**
  Deploy logging solutions like the ELK Stack (Elasticsearch, Logstash, Kibana) or cloud-based services to aggregate logs from all nodes, containers, and workflows. Centralized logging simplifies troubleshooting by providing a single point of reference for all system events.
- **Log Retention and Analysis:**
  Set appropriate log retention policies to balance storage costs with the need for historical data during root cause analysis. Regularly analyze logs to identify recurring issues and trends that may require proactive intervention.

4. User and Business Metrics

- **End-to-End Monitoring:**
  Beyond technical metrics, track business-oriented KPIs such as user response times, conversion rates, and customer satisfaction levels. Integrating these metrics with technical monitoring can provide a holistic view of system performance and its impact on business outcomes.
- **Feedback Integration:**
  Incorporate user feedback and system performance data to continuously refine your workflows. Use this information to adjust thresholds, optimize resource allocation, and improve overall efficiency.

5. Best Practices for Monitoring

- **Automated Monitoring Tools:**
  Implement automation in your monitoring setup to reduce manual

oversight. Automated tools can detect anomalies, trigger alerts, and even initiate corrective actions without human intervention.

- **Regular Audits and Reviews:**
  Schedule periodic reviews of your monitoring strategies to ensure that they remain aligned with evolving workloads and system configurations. Regular audits help you adapt to new challenges and optimize your monitoring setup over time.
- **Integration with CI/CD Pipelines:**
  Integrate monitoring into your CI/CD pipelines to catch performance issues early in the development process. Continuous testing and monitoring ensure that changes do not negatively impact system stability.

Summary

Comprehensive monitoring strategies are the cornerstone of operational excellence in Flowise AI. By implementing real-time system and application monitoring, centralized logging, and robust alerting mechanisms, you can gain deep insights into both technical performance and business impact. These strategies enable proactive troubleshooting, efficient resource management, and continuous improvement, ensuring that your workflows remain reliable, scalable, and aligned with organizational goals.

10.2.1 Real-Time Logging and Alerting

Real-time logging and alerting are essential components of a proactive monitoring strategy, ensuring that issues are identified and addressed as soon as they occur. By continuously capturing and analyzing logs, and triggering alerts based on predefined thresholds, you can maintain high operational reliability and swiftly respond to anomalies. Here's how to effectively implement real-time logging and alerting:

Real-Time Logging

- **Centralized Log Aggregation:**
  - Collect logs from all components of your system—such as application logs, container logs, and system metrics—into a centralized logging platform.
  - Tools like the ELK Stack (Elasticsearch, Logstash, Kibana) or cloud-based logging services enable you to search, filter, and analyze log data in real time.
- **Structured and Consistent Logging:**

- Use structured logging formats (e.g., JSON) to ensure logs are consistently formatted. This standardization simplifies parsing and correlation of events.
- Include essential metadata in each log entry (e.g., timestamps, log levels, component names) to facilitate rapid troubleshooting.
- **Granular Log Levels:**
  - Implement multiple log levels (DEBUG, INFO, WARNING, ERROR, CRITICAL) to capture both routine operations and significant issues.
  - Configure the logging system to escalate critical errors while providing detailed debugging information when needed.

Alerting Mechanisms

- **Threshold-Based Alerts:**
  - Define key performance indicators (KPIs) and thresholds for metrics such as CPU usage, memory consumption, response times, and error rates.
  - Configure alerts to trigger when these thresholds are breached, ensuring that potential issues are flagged immediately.
- **Automated Notification Systems:**
  - Integrate alerting systems with messaging platforms (e.g., Slack, Microsoft Teams, email, SMS) to deliver notifications directly to your team.
  - Automated alerts enable rapid response and minimize the time between issue detection and resolution.
- **Anomaly Detection:**
  - Use advanced monitoring tools that incorporate machine learning to detect abnormal patterns in log data. Anomaly detection can identify subtle issues that might not trigger standard threshold-based alerts.
  - Fine-tune these systems to reduce false positives while ensuring critical events are not missed.

Best Practices

- **Real-Time Dashboards:**
  - Set up dashboards that visualize key log metrics and alert statuses in real time. This provides a comprehensive view of system health and aids in quick decision-making.

- **Automated Incident Response:**
  - Consider integrating automated scripts or runbooks that can perform initial corrective actions based on specific alerts. This helps mitigate issues before they escalate.
- **Regular Review and Tuning:**
  - Continuously review alert thresholds, log retention policies, and notification settings to ensure they remain aligned with evolving system demands and performance metrics.
- **Documentation:**
  - Document your logging and alerting configurations along with response procedures. Clear documentation ensures that team members can quickly understand and act on alerts when they occur.

Summary

Implementing robust real-time logging and alerting strategies is critical for maintaining operational excellence in your Flowise AI deployments. Centralized, structured logging provides the detailed insights needed to diagnose issues, while automated, threshold-based alerts ensure that your team is promptly informed of potential problems. By following these best practices, you can create a proactive monitoring environment that minimizes downtime, enhances system performance, and supports continuous improvement in your AI workflows.

10.2.2 Performance Metrics and Analysis

Performance metrics and analysis form the backbone of understanding how your Flowise AI workflows perform under real-world conditions. By systematically measuring key indicators and analyzing trends over time, you can identify bottlenecks, optimize resource usage, and ensure that your system meets its operational objectives. This section outlines the critical metrics to monitor, methods for analyzing them, and strategies for leveraging this data to drive continuous improvement.

Key Performance Metrics

- **Execution Time:**
  Measure the time taken for each workflow or node execution. Shorter execution times indicate more efficient processing, while prolonged durations may highlight performance issues that need addressing.

- **Resource Utilization:**
  Track CPU, memory, and disk I/O usage across your deployment. High resource consumption on specific nodes can signal inefficiencies or the need for scaling.
- **Throughput:**
  Assess the number of tasks or transactions processed per unit of time. Throughput metrics are essential for understanding system capacity and identifying when performance limits are reached.
- **Latency:**
  Monitor the delay between a request and its corresponding response. Low latency is critical for real-time applications and user satisfaction.
- **Error Rates:**
  Keep track of error frequencies, including failed API calls, node execution errors, or system timeouts. An increase in error rates may indicate underlying issues that require prompt intervention.
- **Scalability Indicators:**
  Analyze how performance metrics change as workload increases. This includes monitoring auto-scaling events, load balancing effectiveness, and the impact of parallel processing on overall efficiency.

Analysis Techniques

- **Trend Analysis:**
  Collect performance data over time to identify trends and seasonal variations. Trend analysis can help forecast when additional resources might be required and assess the impact of optimization efforts.
- **Comparative Benchmarking:**
  Compare performance metrics across different configurations, deployment environments, or versions of your workflows. Benchmarking provides a baseline against which improvements can be measured.
- **Bottleneck Identification:**
  Use metrics to pinpoint specific nodes or processes that slow down the workflow. Once identified, these bottlenecks can be targeted for code optimization, resource reallocation, or architectural adjustments.
- **Correlation Analysis:**
  Examine how different metrics interact—such as how increased memory usage might affect execution time. Correlation analysis helps uncover systemic issues that aren't apparent when metrics are viewed in isolation.

Tools and Techniques

- **Monitoring Dashboards:**
  Utilize tools like Grafana or cloud-native monitoring solutions (AWS CloudWatch, Azure Monitor) to visualize performance metrics in real time. Custom dashboards can provide an at-a-glance view of system health.
- **Profiling Tools:**
  Use profiling tools (e.g., cProfile, memory_profiler) to collect detailed performance data at the code level. This data is invaluable for identifying inefficient algorithms or memory leaks.
- **Automated Reporting:**
  Generate periodic performance reports to document improvements, track regressions, and support decision-making regarding scaling and optimization efforts.

Leveraging Data for Continuous Improvement

- **Iterative Optimization:**
  Use performance data to guide incremental optimizations. For example, if benchmarking reveals a particular node is underperforming, focus on optimizing its code or adjusting its configuration parameters.
- **Resource Planning:**
  Leverage historical performance metrics to inform capacity planning. Understanding resource utilization patterns allows you to proactively scale infrastructure to meet future demands.
- **Feedback Loops:**
  Establish feedback loops where insights from performance analysis drive changes in the workflow configuration. Continuous feedback ensures that your system remains efficient and responsive to evolving requirements.

Summary

Performance metrics and analysis are essential for maintaining operational excellence in Flowise AI deployments. By systematically measuring execution time, resource utilization, throughput, latency, and error rates, and by employing robust analysis techniques, you can uncover inefficiencies and drive continuous improvements. Leveraging these insights with real-time dashboards, profiling tools, and automated reporting ensures that your workflows are optimized for both current performance and future scalability.

10.3 Troubleshooting, Maintenance, and Community Tools

A robust production system doesn't just rely on effective deployment—it also requires ongoing troubleshooting, routine maintenance, and active engagement with community resources. In this section, we outline strategies and tools that help you identify, diagnose, and resolve issues quickly, ensuring long-term system reliability and performance.

Troubleshooting Strategies

- **Root Cause Analysis:**
  - **Systematic Investigation:**
    When issues arise, begin with a systematic investigation. Use centralized logs, error reports, and performance metrics to trace issues back to their source.
  - **Component Isolation:**
    Test individual workflow components or nodes in isolation to identify if the problem originates from a specific area.
- **Automated Alerts:**
  - **Threshold-Based Alerts:**
    Set up automated alerts for critical performance metrics such as high error rates, resource usage spikes, or prolonged execution times.
  - **Real-Time Notifications:**
    Integrate alerting systems with communication tools (e.g., Slack, email) to notify the team immediately when an issue is detected.
- **Incremental Debugging:**
  - **Step-by-Step Execution:**
    Run your workflows incrementally and verify outputs at each stage, making it easier to pinpoint where errors or performance issues occur.
  - **Diagnostic Tools:**
    Utilize built-in debugging tools, breakpoints, and log analysis to isolate problematic behavior.

Maintenance Techniques

- **Regular Updates and Patching:**
  - **Software and Security Updates:**
    Keep Flowise AI and its dependencies up to date to benefit from performance improvements, new features, and security patches.
  - **Infrastructure Maintenance:**
    Schedule regular maintenance windows to apply updates, perform backups, and review system configurations.
- **Automated Backups and Recovery:**
  - **Data Backup:**
    Implement regular backup routines for configurations, databases, and logs to safeguard against data loss.
  - **Disaster Recovery Plans:**
    Develop and test recovery procedures to ensure that you can quickly restore service in case of failures.
- **Performance Monitoring and Tuning:**
  - **Continuous Profiling:**
    Continuously profile workflows to identify and resolve performance bottlenecks.
  - **Iterative Refinement:**
    Use insights from monitoring data to optimize workflows and adjust resource allocation dynamically.

Community Tools and Engagement

- **Documentation and Knowledge Bases:**
  - **Official Documentation:**
    Regularly consult the official Flowise AI documentation for guidance, best practices, and updates on new features.
  - **Community-Contributed Resources:**
    Leverage tutorials, FAQs, and case studies contributed by the community to solve common challenges.
- **Support Forums and Discussion Groups:**
  - **Online Communities:**
    Engage with user forums, GitHub repositories, and dedicated community platforms where developers share solutions, offer advice, and collaborate on troubleshooting issues.
  - **Peer Collaboration:**
    Participating in community discussions can provide new

perspectives on complex issues and accelerate problem-solving.
- **Issue Tracking and Feedback:**
  - **Bug Reporting:**
    Use issue trackers on platforms like GitHub to report bugs, track progress, and contribute fixes.
  - **Feature Requests and Enhancements:**
    Engage with the community to propose and discuss potential improvements or new features that can enhance overall system stability and performance.

Best Practices

- **Proactive Monitoring:**
  Establish automated systems that continuously monitor both technical and business metrics, ensuring that potential issues are identified before they escalate.
- **Comprehensive Documentation:**
  Maintain detailed records of troubleshooting steps, incident logs, and resolution procedures. This documentation serves as a reference for future maintenance and helps standardize the troubleshooting process.
- **Regular Training and Knowledge Sharing:**
  Encourage team members to participate in training sessions and share lessons learned from past incidents. This collective knowledge enhances the team's ability to respond to and resolve issues efficiently.
- **Iterative Improvement:**
  Use the insights gained from troubleshooting and maintenance activities to continuously refine workflows, optimize resource usage, and improve overall system resilience.

Summary

Effective troubleshooting, maintenance, and community engagement are critical for sustaining operational excellence in Flowise AI deployments. By adopting systematic troubleshooting strategies, automating maintenance routines, and actively leveraging community tools and support, you can ensure that your AI workflows remain robust, efficient, and resilient over time. These practices not only help in rapid issue resolution but also contribute to the continuous improvement and evolution of your system in dynamic production environments.

10.3.1 Debugging Techniques and Case Studies

Effective debugging is essential for maintaining the health of your Flowise AI workflows. This section outlines various debugging techniques that help identify and resolve issues quickly, along with real-world case studies that illustrate how these techniques have been successfully applied.

Debugging Techniques

- **Incremental Testing and Isolation:**
  - **Unit Testing:**
    Test individual nodes or components in isolation. This helps verify that each module performs as expected before it's integrated into the larger workflow.
  - **Step-by-Step Execution:**
    Execute your workflow in stages, verifying outputs at each step. Isolating segments of the workflow can reveal which specific part is causing errors.
- **Comprehensive Logging:**
  - **Structured Logs:**
    Use structured logging (e.g., JSON) to capture detailed, timestamped information from each node. Ensure that logs include context such as node identifiers and operation details.
  - **Centralized Log Management:**
    Aggregate logs from all parts of the workflow using centralized logging systems (like the ELK stack or cloud-based logging solutions) to correlate events and quickly pinpoint anomalies.
- **Real-Time Monitoring and Alerts:**
  - **Dashboards:**
    Set up real-time dashboards with tools like Grafana or cloud-native monitors to visualize key performance indicators and error rates.
  - **Automated Alerts:**
    Configure alerts that notify your team immediately when critical thresholds are exceeded or when specific error patterns occur.
- **Diagnostic and Profiling Tools:**
  - **Code Profilers:**
    Utilize tools such as Python's `cProfile` or `line_profiler` to analyze execution times and resource usage. This can reveal inefficient code paths or bottlenecks.

- o **Memory Profiling:**
  Apply memory profiling tools (e.g., `memory_profiler`) to detect leaks or excessive memory consumption, particularly in data-intensive nodes.
- **Iterative Debugging and Reproduction:**
  - o **Simulation of Fault Conditions:**
    Create controlled environments or use simulated inputs to reproduce errors consistently. This iterative debugging helps in narrowing down the root cause.
  - o **Breakpoints and Interactive Debugging:**
    Leverage IDE capabilities to set breakpoints and step through code execution, examining variable states and data flows in detail.

Case Studies

- **Case Study 1: Resolving Data Flow Inconsistencies in a Customer Support Workflow**
  Scenario: A customer support chatbot intermittently returned incorrect responses due to data mismatches.
  Approach:
  - o **Incremental Testing:** Developers isolated the data ingestion and processing nodes to determine which component was misformatting the input data.
  - o **Log Analysis:** Centralized logs revealed that certain data entries were not being normalized correctly before reaching the LLM node.
  - o **Solution:** A data preprocessing checkpoint was added to standardize inputs, and additional unit tests were written to cover edge cases.
    Outcome: The chatbot's accuracy improved significantly, and error rates dropped as the issue was resolved through targeted debugging.
- **Case Study 2: Optimizing Execution Time in a Data Processing Pipeline**
  Scenario: A complex data processing workflow was experiencing high latency, affecting overall system performance.
  Approach:
  - o **Profiling:** Developers used `cProfile` to identify slow-performing nodes.

- o **Bottleneck Identification:** Profiling data revealed that a specific processing node was performing redundant computations.
- o **Optimization:** The node was refactored to utilize vectorized operations with NumPy, reducing the computation time dramatically.
  Outcome: Overall execution time was reduced by over 40%, and the system handled higher loads with improved responsiveness.
- **Case Study 3: Addressing Memory Leaks in a Workflow with High Data Volume**
  Scenario: A workflow processing large datasets began to slow down over time due to memory leaks.
  Approach:
  - o **Memory Profiling:** Tools like `memory_profiler` were used to monitor memory usage across nodes.
  - o **Identifying the Culprit:** Logs and profiler output indicated that a custom node for data transformation was not releasing memory efficiently.
  - o **Solution:** The node's implementation was revised to free up memory after processing each batch, and caching mechanisms were optimized.
    Outcome: The memory footprint stabilized, preventing crashes during extended operations and allowing the system to run continuously under heavy load.

Summary

Debugging techniques such as incremental testing, comprehensive logging, real-time monitoring, and iterative profiling are vital for maintaining robust Flowise AI workflows. The provided case studies demonstrate how these techniques can be applied in practical scenarios—resolving data inconsistencies, optimizing execution time, and addressing memory leaks. By incorporating these debugging strategies into your development and maintenance processes, you can ensure that your AI workflows remain efficient, scalable, and reliable even as they evolve and handle increasing complexities.

10.3.2 Leveraging Community Resources for Support

Harnessing community resources is a key strategy for maintaining, troubleshooting, and evolving your Flowise AI deployments. Engaging with a vibrant community of developers, experts, and users can accelerate problem-solving, inspire innovative solutions, and provide a wealth of shared knowledge. Here's how to effectively leverage community resources for support:

Online Forums and Discussion Groups

- **Developer Forums and Q&A Sites:**
  Participate in dedicated forums, such as the Flowise AI community forum or broader platforms like Stack Overflow. These platforms allow you to ask questions, share experiences, and gain insights from others who have faced similar challenges.
- **Social Media and Messaging Platforms:**
  Join relevant groups on Slack, Discord, or LinkedIn where real-time discussions can lead to rapid troubleshooting and idea exchange. Such communities often host regular discussions or "office hours" with experienced users and developers.

Open-Source Repositories and Code Sharing

- **GitHub and GitLab:**
  Explore repositories related to Flowise AI, including the official repository and community-contributed projects. Reviewing others' code, issues, and pull requests can provide practical insights and ready-made solutions.
- **Code Samples and Tutorials:**
  Take advantage of shared code samples, tutorials, and walkthroughs. Many community members publish blog posts or video tutorials that address common issues or demonstrate advanced customizations.

Documentation and Knowledge Bases

- **Official Documentation:**
  Regularly review and contribute to the Flowise AI documentation. Enhancements and updates from community feedback can clarify common pitfalls and share best practices.
- **Wiki and FAQ Sections:**
  Check community-maintained wikis or FAQ sections that compile solutions for frequently encountered issues. These resources can save time by providing quick answers and actionable advice.

Collaboration and Mentorship

- **Pair Programming and Mentoring:**
  Engage in pair programming sessions or seek mentorship from more experienced community members. Direct collaboration can help you overcome challenging problems faster and gain deeper insights into best practices.
- **Contributing Back:**
  Contribute fixes, enhancements, or documentation improvements back to the community. This not only helps others but also deepens your understanding and builds your reputation as a knowledgeable practitioner.

Conferences and Webinars

- **Industry Conferences:**
  Attend AI and developer conferences where Flowise AI might be featured. These events provide opportunities to network with peers, attend workshops, and learn about emerging trends.
- **Webinars and Virtual Meetups:**
  Participate in webinars and virtual meetups organized by the Flowise AI community. These sessions often cover real-world case studies, troubleshooting tips, and advanced techniques.

Best Practices for Leveraging Community Resources

- **Be Active and Engaged:**
  Regularly contribute to discussions, ask questions, and share your experiences. Active participation helps build a network of trusted contacts and increases the likelihood of receiving timely support.
- **Stay Up-to-Date:**
  Follow the latest updates, changelogs, and community announcements. Keeping abreast of new developments ensures that you can quickly adopt improvements and avoid known issues.
- **Utilize Search and Tags:**
  When seeking support, use search functionalities and relevant tags to quickly locate discussions and solutions that address your issue.
- **Document and Share:**
  Keep your own documentation of resolved issues and solutions. Sharing your learnings not only aids others but also serves as a personal reference for future troubleshooting.

Summary

Leveraging community resources for support is an effective strategy to enhance your Flowise AI experience. By actively participating in forums, collaborating on open-source projects, engaging in mentorship, and attending industry events, you gain access to a rich ecosystem of knowledge and support. This collective wisdom not only helps resolve issues more efficiently but also drives continuous learning and innovation, ultimately contributing to the long-term success of your AI workflows.

Chapter 11: Future Directions and Innovations in Flowise AI

As the field of artificial intelligence continues to evolve at a rapid pace, Flowise AI is positioned to adapt and grow, incorporating cutting-edge technologies and innovative methodologies. This chapter explores emerging trends, anticipated innovations, and strategic directions for the future of Flowise AI. It provides insights into how the platform can evolve to meet new challenges and harness opportunities in an ever-changing technological landscape.

11.1 Emerging Trends in LLMs and AI Workflows

The landscape of artificial intelligence is rapidly evolving, driven largely by advancements in Large Language Models (LLMs) and innovative AI workflow designs. In this section, we explore several emerging trends that are set to shape the future of LLMs and the way AI workflows are built, deployed, and maintained.

Advancements in LLM Architectures

- **Next-Generation Transformers:**
  Innovations in transformer architectures, such as sparse attention mechanisms and efficient scaling techniques, are enabling the development of more powerful yet resource-efficient models. These improvements allow LLMs to process longer contexts and generate more accurate, coherent text.
- **Multi-Modal Models:**
  Future LLMs are increasingly incorporating multi-modal capabilities, processing not only text but also images, audio, and even video. This integration opens up new applications, from enhanced content generation and summarization to more robust human-computer interaction.
- **Personalized and Domain-Specific Models:**
  Fine-tuning and transfer learning techniques are evolving to make it easier to customize LLMs for specific industries or individual users. Personalized models that adapt to particular contexts promise to deliver more relevant and context-aware outputs.

Evolution of AI Workflows

- **Dynamic Workflow Adaptation:**
  AI workflows are moving towards more dynamic and adaptive
  systems. Instead of static, pre-defined processes, future workflows
  may automatically adjust configurations, allocate resources, or even
  re-route tasks based on real-time performance metrics and
  environmental changes.
- **Integration of Retrieval-Augmented Generation (RAG):**
  The fusion of data retrieval techniques with generative models is
  becoming increasingly important. By leveraging up-to-date external
  data sources, RAG systems can mitigate issues like hallucinations
  and provide responses that are both contextually rich and factually
  accurate.
- **Agentic and Decentralized Workflows:**
  The rise of agentic workflows, where autonomous agents handle
  discrete tasks and collaborate dynamically, is set to transform how
  complex AI systems are designed. These decentralized architectures
  enhance scalability, fault tolerance, and adaptability, enabling
  systems to operate efficiently in distributed environments.

Efficiency and Sustainability

- **Energy-Efficient Models:**
  With growing concerns about the environmental impact of large-scale
  AI, research is focusing on developing models that are more energy-
  efficient. Techniques like model pruning, quantization, and
  distillation are being refined to reduce computational costs without
  sacrificing performance.
- **Edge AI Integration:**
  As hardware continues to improve, there is a trend towards deploying
  AI workflows on edge devices. This shift allows for real-time
  processing with reduced latency and bandwidth usage, enabling
  applications in IoT, autonomous vehicles, and smart cities.

Collaborative and Open-Source Innovation

- **Community-Driven Development:**
  Open-source communities are playing an increasingly vital role in
  advancing LLM technologies and AI workflow methodologies.
  Collaborative platforms and shared repositories facilitate rapid

innovation and the dissemination of best practices across the industry.

- **Interoperability and Standardization:**
  Efforts to standardize APIs, data formats, and integration protocols are underway, which will simplify the process of combining various AI components into cohesive workflows. Greater interoperability ensures that organizations can mix and match technologies from different providers seamlessly.

Summary

Emerging trends in LLMs and AI workflows are paving the way for more powerful, adaptive, and sustainable AI systems. Advances in transformer architectures, multi-modal processing, and personalized models are enhancing the capabilities of LLMs, while dynamic, agentic workflows and retrieval-augmented approaches are transforming how AI applications are designed and executed. Additionally, a strong focus on energy efficiency, edge computing, and community collaboration is setting the stage for an AI ecosystem that is both innovative and responsible. As these trends converge, they promise to unlock new possibilities and drive the next wave of AI advancements.

11.2 The Next Frontier: Advanced Agentic Workflows

As AI systems grow in complexity and scale, traditional agentic workflows are evolving into more advanced, self-optimizing ecosystems. Advanced agentic workflows represent the next frontier in decentralized AI systems, where autonomous agents not only perform specialized tasks but also dynamically adapt, collaborate, and even learn from their environment. This section explores emerging concepts, technological innovations, and potential applications that are driving the evolution of agentic workflows.

Key Innovations in Advanced Agentic Workflows

- **Dynamic Coordination and Orchestration:**
  Future agentic systems will feature more sophisticated coordination mechanisms that enable agents to reconfigure their roles and data flows in real time. Advanced scheduling algorithms and decentralized decision-making protocols will allow agents to:

- **Adapt to changing conditions:** Automatically adjust priorities, resource allocation, or task assignments based on real-time performance metrics and environmental changes.
- **Collaborate seamlessly:** Leverage peer-to-peer communication and consensus algorithms to coordinate tasks without relying on a centralized controller.

- **Self-Optimizing Agents:**
Agents are expected to evolve into self-learning entities that optimize their performance over time. By integrating reinforcement learning or other adaptive algorithms, agents can:
  - **Improve efficiency:** Learn optimal strategies for data processing and decision-making by continuously evaluating feedback from previous tasks.
  - **Enhance fault tolerance:** Predict and mitigate potential failures through proactive adjustments, ensuring that the overall system remains resilient.

- **Hybrid Centralized-Decentralized Architectures:**
While fully decentralized systems offer flexibility and scalability, a hybrid approach can provide the best of both worlds. In these architectures:
  - **Central oversight:** A lightweight central coordinator or meta-agent may monitor overall system health and mediate resource distribution without micromanaging individual tasks.
  - **Decentralized execution:** Autonomous agents continue to operate independently, ensuring that localized decision-making remains fast and responsive.

- **Integration of Multi-Modal Data and Analytics:**
Advanced workflows are increasingly incorporating multi-modal data—from text and images to sensor streams and real-time video—into a unified processing framework. This integration enables agents to:
  - **Enrich context:** Fuse diverse data types to provide a more comprehensive understanding of complex scenarios.
  - **Drive innovation:** Open up new applications in areas like augmented reality, autonomous systems, and smart city management.

Benefits of Advanced Agentic Workflows

- **Enhanced Scalability and Resilience:**
By dynamically adapting to workload variations and environmental changes, advanced agentic workflows offer unparalleled scalability.

Self-optimizing agents can quickly recover from failures, ensuring high system uptime and robust performance even under stress.

- **Improved Decision-Making:**
  With real-time adaptive coordination and multi-modal data integration, these workflows deliver more accurate and context-aware outputs. This leads to better-informed decisions and more efficient automation in complex domains.
- **Cost Efficiency and Resource Optimization:**
  Dynamic scaling and adaptive resource allocation mean that computational resources are used more efficiently, reducing operational costs while maintaining high performance.

Real-World Applications and Future Directions

- **Autonomous Supply Chain Management:**
  Advanced agentic workflows can manage complex supply chains by dynamically adjusting logistics, inventory levels, and demand forecasting in response to real-time market conditions.
- **Smart Cities and IoT Integration:**
  In smart city environments, decentralized agents can coordinate traffic management, energy distribution, and public safety systems. These workflows will use real-time data from diverse sensors to optimize urban operations continuously.
- **Next-Generation Customer Support:**
  Imagine a customer support system where agents not only handle routine inquiries but also collaborate to escalate complex issues, all while learning from each interaction to improve service quality over time.

Summary

Advanced agentic workflows mark a transformative step in the evolution of AI systems. By integrating dynamic coordination, self-optimization, and hybrid architectures, these next-generation workflows promise to deliver enhanced scalability, resilience, and efficiency. As they incorporate multi-modal data and advanced analytics, they will unlock new applications and drive innovation across industries. Embracing these advancements will position Flowise AI at the forefront of modern AI technology, paving the way for smarter, more adaptive, and cost-effective solutions.

11.3 The Roadmap for Flowise AI

The roadmap for Flowise AI outlines the strategic milestones and future enhancements designed to propel the platform into the next era of AI development. This roadmap is driven by both emerging technological trends and community feedback, ensuring that Flowise AI remains adaptable, scalable, and at the forefront of AI innovation.

Short-Term Goals

- **Enhanced Integration with Emerging LLMs:**
  - Expand support for next-generation language models and multi-modal AI architectures.
  - Provide flexible APIs and built-in nodes to easily incorporate fine-tuned, domain-specific models.
- **Modular Plugin Ecosystem:**
  - Develop an enriched plugin architecture that enables seamless addition, removal, or update of functionalities.
  - Foster community contributions by offering streamlined tools and documentation for plugin development.
- **User Interface Enhancements:**
  - Upgrade the visual workflow builder with interactive, real-time data flow visualizations.
  - Improve usability with intuitive dashboards and simplified configuration interfaces to reduce the learning curve.
- **Performance and Scalability Improvements:**
  - Integrate advanced caching, parallel processing, and dynamic resource allocation strategies.
  - Optimize container orchestration through enhanced support for Kubernetes and cloud-native deployments.

Long-Term Vision

- **Decentralized and Agentic Architectures:**
  - Transition toward fully decentralized workflows where autonomous agents dynamically collaborate and self-optimize.
  - Explore hybrid models that combine centralized oversight with decentralized execution for improved efficiency and resilience.
- **Edge AI and Federated Learning:**

- o Enable Flowise AI to operate on edge devices, reducing latency and supporting real-time applications in IoT and smart city scenarios.
  - o Incorporate federated learning methodologies to facilitate privacy-preserving model training across decentralized data sources.
- **Multi-Modal Data Processing:**
  - o Extend the platform to natively support multi-modal data (e.g., text, image, audio, video), enabling richer, context-aware AI applications.
  - o Develop advanced nodes and integrations to process and fuse multi-modal inputs into unified workflows.
- **Explainable and Responsible AI:**
  - o Integrate advanced explainability tools to help users understand model decisions and ensure compliance with emerging regulatory standards.
  - o Foster a culture of ethical AI by embedding responsible usage guidelines and transparency measures into the platform.

Community and Ecosystem Development

- **Open-Source Collaboration:**
  - o Continue to leverage and grow the Flowise AI open-source community, encouraging shared innovations and collaborative problem-solving.
  - o Regularly incorporate community feedback to guide feature development and improvements.
- **Continuous Learning and Adaptation:**
  - o Establish mechanisms for continuous integration of cutting-edge research, ensuring that Flowise AI evolves alongside advancements in the broader AI field.
  - o Promote workshops, webinars, and collaborative projects to keep the community engaged and informed about new developments.

Summary

The roadmap for Flowise AI sets a clear path forward that combines immediate enhancements with visionary long-term goals. In the short term, the focus is on integrating advanced LLMs, enriching the plugin ecosystem, and refining the user interface for improved usability and performance. Looking ahead, Flowise AI aims to embrace decentralized architectures, support edge computing and federated learning, process multi-modal data, and champion explainable and responsible AI practices. By actively engaging with the community and continuously incorporating the latest research, Flowise AI is poised to remain a dynamic, innovative platform that meets the evolving needs of modern AI applications.

11.3.1 Planned Enhancements and Community Contributions

The future of Flowise AI is shaped not only by strategic internal planning but also by the vibrant contributions of its community. This section outlines the planned enhancements for upcoming releases and highlights how community input is integrated into the development process.

Planned Enhancements

- **Expanded Model Integration:**
  Future versions will include support for emerging LLMs and multi-modal models, enabling smoother integration with next-generation language and vision systems. Enhanced API endpoints and pre-configured nodes will allow users to leverage these models with minimal setup.
- **Enhanced Plugin Ecosystem:**
  Flowise AI is set to introduce a more robust and user-friendly plugin architecture. Planned enhancements include:
  - A dedicated marketplace for community-developed plugins.
  - Simplified tools and documentation to streamline plugin development.
  - Improved interoperability between custom plugins and core functionalities.
- **Advanced User Interface Improvements:**
  Upcoming updates will focus on refining the visual workflow builder by incorporating:
  - Interactive, real-time data flow visualizations.
  - Intuitive dashboards that offer deeper insights into workflow performance.
  - A more streamlined and customizable user experience to reduce the learning curve for new users.
- **Performance and Scalability Optimizations:**
  To address the growing demands of production environments, future releases will incorporate:
  - Advanced caching strategies and parallel processing techniques.

- o Enhanced support for container orchestration tools like Kubernetes.
  - o Dynamic resource allocation features that adapt to workload fluctuations in real time.
- **Decentralized and Agentic Workflow Enhancements:**
  Building on the current agentic workflow model, planned improvements will:
  - o Introduce mechanisms for more dynamic coordination among autonomous agents.
  - o Integrate self-optimization features that allow agents to learn and adapt over time.
  - o Explore hybrid centralized-decentralized architectures for improved efficiency and fault tolerance.

Community Contributions

- **Open-Source Collaboration:**
  The Flowise AI community plays a critical role in its evolution. Community contributions include:
  - o Code enhancements, bug fixes, and performance improvements submitted via GitHub.
  - o User-generated plugins, custom nodes, and integrations that extend the platform's capabilities.
  - o Active participation in discussion forums, webinars, and community meetups that inform the roadmap.
- **Feedback-Driven Development:**
  Community feedback is actively solicited and integrated into the planning process:
  - o Regular surveys and feedback sessions help prioritize new features and identify pain points.
  - o Beta testing programs enable users to provide early feedback on upcoming releases, ensuring that enhancements align with real-world needs.
  - o Transparent issue tracking and public roadmaps allow the community to monitor progress and contribute ideas.
- **Documentation and Knowledge Sharing:**
  Community members also contribute to a rich ecosystem of tutorials, guides, and best practice documents:
  - o Shared experiences and use-case studies are aggregated to create a comprehensive knowledge base.
  - o Collaborative platforms and open documentation efforts foster continuous learning and innovation.

Summary

Planned enhancements for Flowise AI focus on expanding model integration, enriching the plugin ecosystem, refining the user interface, and optimizing performance and scalability. Simultaneously, the platform's future is being actively shaped by community contributions, which drive innovation through collaborative development, feedback-driven improvements, and shared knowledge. Together, these efforts ensure that Flowise AI evolves into a more powerful, flexible, and user-centric platform, poised to meet the dynamic demands of modern AI applications.

11.3.2 Integrating New Technologies (Edge AI, IoT, etc.)

As the AI landscape evolves, integrating new technologies such as edge computing and IoT is becoming critical to harness real-time, localized intelligence. Flowise AI is poised to embrace these advancements, enabling deployments that are both efficient and context-aware. This section outlines strategies and considerations for integrating emerging technologies with Flowise AI.

Embracing Edge AI

- **Localized Processing:**
  Edge AI involves processing data on local devices rather than transmitting it to centralized data centers. This approach reduces latency, conserves bandwidth, and improves responsiveness, especially in time-sensitive applications.
- **Integration Strategies:**
  - **Model Compression:**
    Utilize techniques like quantization, pruning, or distillation to compress large LLMs so they can run effectively on edge devices.
  - **Hybrid Workflows:**
    Combine edge processing for initial data analysis with cloud-based Flowise AI workflows for more resource-intensive tasks. This hybrid approach enables real-time decision-making while leveraging the power of centralized AI when necessary.
  - **Deployment Frameworks:**
    Use containerization (e.g., Docker) and lightweight orchestration frameworks (e.g., K3s, a lightweight Kubernetes distribution) to deploy Flowise AI on edge devices.

Leveraging IoT Integration

- **Real-Time Data Collection:**
  IoT devices generate vast amounts of sensor data that can be invaluable for AI workflows. Flowise AI can be integrated with IoT platforms to ingest, process, and analyze data in real time.
- **Integration Strategies:**
  - **APIs and Webhooks:**
    Configure Flowise AI nodes to receive data from IoT devices via APIs or webhooks. This data can be used to trigger workflows, update models, or generate insights.
  - **Edge Gateways:**
    Deploy edge gateways that aggregate and preprocess data from multiple IoT devices before sending it to Flowise AI. This reduces network load and ensures that only relevant, filtered data is processed.
  - **Security and Data Privacy:**
    Implement robust security measures, such as TLS encryption and secure authentication, to protect IoT data and ensure compliance with data privacy regulations.

Integrating Other Emerging Technologies

- **Multi-Modal Data Processing:**
  Future AI applications will increasingly require the fusion of diverse data types (e.g., text, images, audio, and video). Flowise AI can expand its capabilities by integrating modules that process and combine multi-modal data, opening up new use cases in fields like augmented reality, automated surveillance, and interactive customer support.
- **5G and Enhanced Connectivity:**
  With the rollout of 5G networks, the high-speed, low-latency connectivity will further enable distributed AI systems. Flowise AI can leverage this enhanced connectivity to support real-time data transfer between edge devices and cloud-based workflows, improving the performance of applications such as remote monitoring and autonomous vehicles.
- **Federated Learning:**
  As concerns over data privacy and security grow, federated learning offers a method for training AI models across decentralized devices without sharing raw data. Integrating federated learning with Flowise

AI can enable collaborative model training in sensitive environments, such as healthcare or finance, where data privacy is paramount.

Best Practices for Integration

- **Modular Architecture:**
  Design your workflows with modularity in mind, allowing easy integration of new technologies as plugins or extensions. This facilitates incremental adoption without disrupting existing systems.
- **Scalability and Flexibility:**
  Ensure that your infrastructure can scale horizontally to accommodate the added complexity and data loads from IoT and edge devices. Employ dynamic resource allocation and auto-scaling mechanisms.
- **Robust Security:**
  Prioritize data encryption, secure authentication, and regular security audits to protect sensitive information as you integrate distributed and edge technologies.
- **Continuous Testing and Monitoring:**
  Implement comprehensive testing strategies to validate the performance of new integrations under real-world conditions. Use real-time monitoring tools to track system performance and quickly identify any issues that arise.

Summary

Integrating new technologies such as Edge AI, IoT, and multi-modal data processing represents a significant opportunity to enhance Flowise AI's versatility and real-world applicability. By leveraging localized processing, robust IoT connectivity, and emerging paradigms like federated learning, Flowise AI can deliver faster, more context-aware, and secure AI workflows. Adhering to best practices in modular design, scalability, security, and continuous monitoring ensures that these integrations contribute effectively to an innovative and future-proof AI ecosystem.

11.4 How to Contribute and Stay Updated

Staying engaged with the Flowise AI ecosystem is key to leveraging the latest innovations and contributing to its evolution. Whether you're a developer, researcher, or enthusiast, there are numerous ways to contribute to Flowise AI and keep abreast of emerging trends.

Contributing to Flowise AI

- **Open-Source Contributions:**
  - **Code Contributions:**
    Review the official GitHub repository, submit bug fixes, propose enhancements, or develop new features. Contributing code not only improves the platform but also helps you build expertise and gain recognition within the community.
  - **Documentation:**
    Help maintain and expand the official documentation. Clear, comprehensive documentation benefits everyone, and your contributions can guide new users and developers.
  - **Plugin and Node Development:**
    Share custom plugins, nodes, and integrations that extend Flowise AI's functionality. Your work can serve as a blueprint for others and foster a collaborative spirit.
  - **Issue Reporting and Feedback:**
    Actively report bugs, suggest improvements, and participate in discussions. Constructive feedback is crucial for identifying pain points and prioritizing future enhancements.
- **Community Engagement:**
  - **Discussion Forums and Social Media:**
    Join community forums, Slack channels, Discord servers, or LinkedIn groups dedicated to Flowise AI. Engaging in these conversations can help you learn from peers, exchange ideas, and stay informed about upcoming features and events.
  - **Webinars and Workshops:**
    Attend or host webinars, virtual meetups, and workshops. These events provide opportunities to share insights, demonstrate new techniques, and learn about best practices.
  - **Conferences and Hackathons:**
    Participate in industry conferences and hackathons where Flowise AI is featured. These events often showcase real-world use cases, advanced integrations, and collaborative projects that can inspire your work.

Staying Updated

- **Official Channels:**
  - **Website and Blog:**
    Regularly visit the Flowise AI website and blog for

announcements, release notes, and detailed articles on new features and improvements.

- o **Documentation Updates:**
  Keep an eye on the official documentation repository for updates and new guidelines that reflect the latest changes.
- o **Newsletter:**
  Subscribe to the Flowise AI newsletter to receive curated updates, community highlights, and upcoming events directly in your inbox.

- **Social Media and Developer Platforms:**
  - o Follow Flowise AI on Twitter, LinkedIn, and GitHub to stay informed about ongoing developments, community contributions, and trending topics.
  - o Join developer communities on platforms like Reddit and Stack Overflow, where you can discuss issues, share projects, and learn from the experiences of others.

- **Release Cycles and Roadmaps:**
  - o Monitor the public roadmap and release schedules to understand what features and enhancements are planned. This insight helps you plan your contributions and adjust your projects to leverage new capabilities as they become available.

Summary

Contributing to and staying updated with Flowise AI is a collaborative, ongoing process that benefits both individual contributors and the entire community. By actively participating in open-source projects, engaging with community channels, and following official updates, you not only enhance your own expertise but also help shape the future of Flowise AI. Embracing these practices ensures that you remain at the forefront of AI innovation while contributing to a dynamic, supportive ecosystem.

Appendices

The appendices provide supplemental information that supports and enhances the content presented throughout the book. They serve as quick reference guides, detailed technical resources, and additional reading materials to help you maximize your understanding and application of Flowise AI. Below is an overview of the key appendices included in this guide:

Appendix A: Glossary of Terms

This glossary provides concise definitions and explanations for key terms, acronyms, and concepts used throughout the book. It is designed as a quick reference to help you understand the technical language and foundational ideas behind Flowise AI and its related technologies.

- **Flowise AI:**
  A platform for building, managing, and deploying AI workflows that integrate large language models (LLMs), retrieval-augmented generation (RAG) systems, and agentic workflows through a visual, node-based interface.
- **LLM (Large Language Model):**
  A deep learning model trained on vast amounts of text data, capable of understanding, generating, and transforming human-like text. Examples include OpenAI's GPT series and Google's BERT.
- **RAG (Retrieval-Augmented Generation):**
  A hybrid approach that combines generative models (LLMs) with data retrieval techniques. RAG systems fetch relevant documents or data to provide context, enhancing the accuracy and factual grounding of generated outputs.
- **Agentic Workflows:**
  Workflows structured as a collection of autonomous agents—each performing a specific task—that collaborate to achieve complex objectives. This modular design improves scalability, fault tolerance, and efficiency.
- **Node:**
  A basic building block in the Flowise AI workflow. Nodes represent discrete operations, such as data ingestion, processing, or output. They can be configured, customized, and connected to form complex workflows.

- **Workflow:**
A complete sequence of interconnected nodes that defines a specific process or task within Flowise AI. Workflows can be simple or complex, incorporating various types of nodes and agentic interactions.
- **Docker:**
A platform for containerization that packages an application along with its dependencies into lightweight, portable containers, ensuring consistency across different environments.
- **Kubernetes:**
An orchestration tool for managing containerized applications. Kubernetes automates deployment, scaling, and management of Docker containers, enabling robust and scalable production environments.
- **CI/CD (Continuous Integration/Continuous Deployment):**
A set of practices and tools that automate the testing, integration, and deployment of code changes. CI/CD pipelines help ensure that updates are deployed smoothly and reliably, reducing downtime and minimizing errors.
- **API (Application Programming Interface):**
A set of protocols and tools for building software applications. The Flowise API provides endpoints for managing workflows, nodes, logs, and other components, enabling seamless integration with external systems.
- **Containerization:**
The process of encapsulating an application and its dependencies into a container that can run uniformly on any platform. Containerization is key to achieving portability and scalability in modern software deployments.
- **Orchestration:**
The automated arrangement, coordination, and management of complex software systems, particularly containerized applications. Tools like Kubernetes manage the deployment, scaling, and operation of these systems.
- **Monitoring:**
The practice of continuously tracking system performance metrics (such as CPU, memory, latency, and error rates) to ensure that applications run efficiently and to detect potential issues before they escalate.
- **Logging:**
The process of recording events, errors, and operational data from an

application. Structured, centralized logging helps in troubleshooting and performance analysis.

- **Edge AI:**
  AI technologies deployed on edge devices (e.g., smartphones, IoT devices) to perform processing locally rather than in centralized data centers. This reduces latency and bandwidth usage while enabling real-time decision-making.

- **Federated Learning:**
  A distributed machine learning approach where models are trained across multiple decentralized devices or servers holding local data samples, without exchanging them. This enhances data privacy and security.

- **Plugin/Extension:**
  Custom modules or add-ons developed to extend the core functionality of Flowise AI. Plugins allow users to integrate additional features or external services seamlessly.

- **DevOps:**
  A set of practices that combine software development (Dev) and IT operations (Ops) aimed at shortening development cycles and ensuring continuous delivery with high software quality.

This glossary is intended to serve as a handy reference for both new and experienced users of Flowise AI, ensuring clarity and consistency in understanding the technical concepts presented throughout the book.

Appendix B: Detailed API Reference and Code Samples

This appendix provides a comprehensive technical reference for the Flowise API, including detailed descriptions of API endpoints, required parameters, expected responses, and sample code snippets. It is designed as a practical guide to help developers integrate, customize, and extend Flowise AI in their own applications.

1. API Overview

- **Architecture:**
  Flowise AI's API follows a RESTful, resource-oriented design. Each endpoint corresponds to a specific resource (e.g., workflows, nodes,

logs) and supports standard HTTP methods such as GET, POST, PUT, and DELETE.

- **Data Format:**
  JSON is used as the standard data exchange format for both requests and responses. Consistent use of JSON ensures interoperability across different programming environments.
- **Authentication:**
  All API calls require authentication via API keys or bearer tokens. Ensure that your requests include an `Authorization` header with the correct credentials.
- **Security:**
  Communication with the API is secured using HTTPS. Always verify that your requests are transmitted securely.

---

2. API Endpoints

2.1 Workflow Management

- **List Workflows:**
  Endpoint: `GET /v1/workflows`
  Description: Retrieves a list of all workflows configured in your Flowise AI instance.
  Parameters:
  - Optional filters (e.g., status, creation date) may be applied as query parameters.
    Example Response:

```json
json
Copy code
[
    {
        "workflow_id": "workflow_12345",
        "name": "Customer Support Chatbot",
        "status": "active",
        "created_at": "2025-03-01T12:00:00Z"
    },
    {
        "workflow_id": "workflow_67890",
        "name": "Data Processing Pipeline",
        "status": "inactive",
        "created_at": "2025-02-15T09:30:00Z"
    }
```

216

]

- **Create a Workflow:**
  Endpoint: `POST /v1/workflows`
  Description: Creates a new workflow.
  Payload Example:

```json
Copy code
{
    "name": "New Workflow",
    "description": "A workflow for processing customer orders",
    "configuration": { ... }
}
```

  Expected Response:

```json
Copy code
{
    "workflow_id": "workflow_abcdef",
    "message": "Workflow created successfully."
}
```

- **Trigger a Workflow:**
  Endpoint: `POST /v1/workflow/run`
  Description: Triggers the execution of a specified workflow with given input data.
  Payload Example:

```json
Copy code
{
    "workflow_id": "workflow_12345",
    "input_data": {
        "user_query": "How do I reset my password?"
    }
}
```

  Expected Response:

```json
Copy code
{
    "execution_id": "exec_001122",
    "status": "started",
```

217

```
    "message": "Workflow execution initiated."
}
```

2.2 Node Management

- **Update Node Configuration:**
  Endpoint: `PUT /v1/node/update`
  Description: Updates the configuration of a specific node within a workflow.
  Payload Example:

```json
Copy code
{
    "node_id": "node_67890",
    "config": {
        "parameter_1": "new_value",
        "parameter_2": 10
    }
}
```

Expected Response:

```json
Copy code
{
    "message": "Node configuration updated
successfully."
}
```

2.3 Log Retrieval

- **Retrieve Workflow Logs:**
  Endpoint: `GET /v1/workflow/logs`
  Description: Retrieves logs associated with a specific workflow execution.
  Query Parameters:
    o `execution_id`: The unique identifier for the workflow execution.
      Example Request:
      `GET /v1/workflow/logs?execution_id=exec_001122`
      Expected Response:

```json
Copy code
```

```json
{
    "logs": [
        {"timestamp": "2025-03-01T12:00:01Z", "level":
"INFO", "message": "Workflow started."},
        {"timestamp": "2025-03-01T12:00:05Z", "level":
"INFO", "message": "Node 'Data Input' completed."},
        {"timestamp": "2025-03-01T12:00:10Z", "level":
"ERROR", "message": "Node 'Processing' encountered an
error."}
    ]
}
```

3. Code Samples

3.1 Retrieving a List of Workflows

```python
python
Copy code
import requests

# Define API endpoint and API key
api_url = "https://api.flowiseai.com/v1/workflows"
api_key = "YOUR_API_KEY_HERE"

# Set headers with authentication
headers = {
    "Content-Type": "application/json",
    "Authorization": f"Bearer {api_key}"
}

# Make the GET request
response = requests.get(api_url, headers=headers)

if response.status_code == 200:
    workflows = response.json()
    print("Workflows:", workflows)
else:
    print("Error retrieving workflows:",
response.status_code, response.text)
```

3.2 Triggering a Workflow

```python
python
Copy code
import requests

# Define API endpoint for triggering a workflow
api_url = "https://api.flowiseai.com/v1/workflow/run"
```

```python
api_key = "YOUR_API_KEY_HERE"

# Configure headers for authentication
headers = {
    "Content-Type": "application/json",
    "Authorization": f"Bearer {api_key}"
}

# Define payload with workflow ID and input data
payload = {
    "workflow_id": "workflow_12345",
    "input_data": {
        "user_query": "How do I reset my password?"
    }
}

# Make the POST request to trigger the workflow
response = requests.post(api_url, json=payload,
headers=headers)

if response.status_code == 200:
    run_status = response.json()
    print("Workflow Triggered Successfully:", run_status)
else:
    print("Error triggering workflow:", response.status_code,
response.text)
```

3.3 Updating Node Configuration

```python
python
Copy code
import requests

# Define API endpoint for updating node configuration
api_url = "https://api.flowiseai.com/v1/node/update"
api_key = "YOUR_API_KEY_HERE"

# Set up headers
headers = {
    "Content-Type": "application/json",
    "Authorization": f"Bearer {api_key}"
}

# Create payload with node ID and new configuration settings
payload = {
    "node_id": "node_67890",
    "config": {
        "parameter_1": "new_value",
        "parameter_2": 10
    }
```

```
}

# Make the PUT request to update the node configuration
response = requests.put(api_url, json=payload,
headers=headers)

if response.status_code == 200:
    update_status = response.json()
    print("Node Configuration Updated:", update_status)
else:
    print("Error updating node configuration:",
response.status_code, response.text)
```

3.4 Retrieving Execution Logs

```python
python
Copy code
import requests

# Define API endpoint for retrieving workflow logs
api_url = "https://api.flowiseai.com/v1/workflow/logs"
api_key = "YOUR_API_KEY_HERE"

# Set headers with authentication
headers = {
    "Content-Type": "application/json",
    "Authorization": f"Bearer {api_key}"
}

# Specify query parameters with execution ID
params = {
    "execution_id": "exec_001122"
}

# Make the GET request to retrieve logs
response = requests.get(api_url, headers=headers,
params=params)

if response.status_code == 200:
    logs = response.json()
    print("Execution Logs:", logs)
else:
    print("Error retrieving logs:", response.status_code,
response.text)
```

4. Additional Resources

- **API Documentation:**
  For more detailed information about each endpoint, parameters, and expected responses, refer to the official Flowise AI API documentation available on the website.
- **Community Contributions:**
  Explore community repositories and forums for additional code examples, custom integrations, and troubleshooting tips.
- **FAQs and Troubleshooting Guides:**
  Consult Appendix C for common issues and detailed troubleshooting steps related to API interactions.

Summary

Appendix B provides a detailed API reference and code samples that serve as practical guides for integrating and extending Flowise AI. Whether you're managing workflows, updating configurations, or retrieving logs, these examples illustrate the effective use of the Flowise API. By leveraging these resources, developers can build custom integrations and automate processes, ultimately enhancing the versatility and efficiency of their AI workflows.

Appendix C: Troubleshooting Guide and FAQs

This appendix serves as a comprehensive resource for diagnosing and resolving common issues encountered when using Flowise AI. It provides step-by-step troubleshooting procedures, practical tips for resolving frequent problems, and a curated list of frequently asked questions (FAQs) to help users quickly find answers and solutions.

Troubleshooting Guide

1. Identifying and Isolating Issues

- **Step-by-Step Execution:**
  Run your workflow incrementally, verifying outputs at each stage.

Isolate specific nodes or components to determine where errors or performance issues occur.

- **Logging and Monitoring:**
  - **Centralized Logs:** Ensure that logs from all nodes are aggregated in a centralized logging system. Review log entries for error messages, warnings, and unusual behavior.
  - **Real-Time Dashboards:** Use tools like Grafana or cloud-native monitors to observe system metrics (e.g., CPU, memory, latency) and quickly detect anomalies.
- **Profiling:**
  Utilize code profilers (e.g., cProfile, memory_profiler) to pinpoint bottlenecks or memory leaks within individual nodes.

2. Common Troubleshooting Scenarios

- **Workflow Execution Failures:**
  - **Issue:** A workflow fails to complete or returns an error message.
  - **Steps to Resolve:**
    1. Check centralized logs for error details and timestamps.
    2. Isolate and test the failing node independently.
    3. Verify input data formats and validate configuration settings.
    4. Confirm that all required dependencies are installed and updated.
- **Performance Bottlenecks:**
  - **Issue:** Slow execution times or high resource consumption.
  - **Steps to Resolve:**
    1. Profile the workflow to identify slow-running nodes.
    2. Optimize data preprocessing and transformation steps.
    3. Consider implementing parallel processing or asynchronous operations.
    4. Check resource allocation and adjust CPU/memory limits if using container orchestration.
- **Data Inconsistencies:**
  - **Issue:** Output data does not match expected results or contains errors.
  - **Steps to Resolve:**
    1. Validate that input data is correctly formatted and normalized.

2. Review node configurations to ensure transformations are applied correctly.
3. Run unit tests on custom nodes to catch logic errors.
4. Compare logs before and after processing steps to locate discrepancies.

- **Integration Failures:**
  - **Issue:** API calls or external integrations are not functioning as expected.
  - **Steps to Resolve:**
    1. Verify API credentials and ensure secure HTTPS connections.
    2. Check endpoint URLs and review any error messages returned by external services.
    3. Test API calls independently using tools like Postman.
    4. Inspect network logs for connectivity issues.

3. Frequently Asked Questions (FAQs)

- **Q: Why is my workflow execution time longer than expected?**
  A: Long execution times may be due to inefficient node configurations, unoptimized data transformations, or resource constraints. Use profiling tools to identify bottlenecks and consider parallel or asynchronous processing.
- **Q: How can I reduce memory usage in my workflows?**
  A: Optimize data handling by cleaning and preprocessing inputs early, use efficient data structures, and implement caching strategies to avoid redundant computations. Profiling with memory_profiler can help identify specific areas for improvement.
- **Q: What should I do if a node consistently fails during execution?**
  A: Isolate the node and run it with controlled, simulated inputs to reproduce the issue. Review logs for error details, check configuration settings, and ensure all dependencies are correctly installed. Consider adding error-handling routines to gracefully manage exceptions.
- **Q: How do I troubleshoot API integration issues?**
  A: Verify that your API keys and tokens are correct and securely stored. Ensure that the API endpoints are correct and that HTTPS is used for secure communication. Use tools like Postman to test API requests independently and review any returned error messages for clues.
- **Q: Where can I find more detailed documentation on specific error messages?**

A: Detailed error information is typically available in the centralized logs. Additionally, refer to the official Flowise AI documentation and community forums, where similar issues are often discussed and resolved.

Best Practices for Troubleshooting

- **Document Incidents:**
  Keep a log of issues encountered, along with the steps taken to resolve them. This documentation can serve as a reference for future troubleshooting and continuous improvement.
- **Iterative Testing:**
  Adopt an iterative approach to testing and debugging. Make incremental changes and validate their impact before proceeding further.
- **Leverage Community Support:**
  Engage with the Flowise AI community through forums, GitHub issues, and social media channels. Sharing your experiences and solutions can accelerate problem resolution and help others facing similar challenges.
- **Regular Maintenance:**
  Schedule regular system audits, performance reviews, and security checks to proactively identify and address potential issues before they impact production.

Summary

Appendix C provides a thorough troubleshooting guide and FAQ section designed to help you quickly diagnose and resolve common issues in Flowise AI. By following systematic troubleshooting steps, leveraging comprehensive logging and monitoring tools, and engaging with community resources, you can ensure that your workflows remain robust and efficient. This proactive approach not only minimizes downtime but also contributes to the continuous improvement and evolution of your AI systems.

Appendix D: Additional Case Studies and Use Cases

This appendix presents a collection of detailed case studies and use cases that illustrate how Flowise AI can be applied in a variety of real-world scenarios. These examples extend beyond the primary use cases discussed in earlier chapters, offering insights into innovative applications across different industries and contexts. Each case study highlights the problem addressed, the workflow design, and the outcomes achieved, serving as a practical resource to inspire and guide your own implementations.

Case Study 1: Healthcare – Patient Data Analysis and Reporting

Objective:
Automate the aggregation, analysis, and reporting of patient data to support clinical decision-making.

Workflow Overview:

- **Data Ingestion:**
  Retrieve patient records and medical imaging data from hospital databases and electronic health records (EHRs) using dedicated input nodes.
- **Data Processing:**
  Utilize processing nodes to clean and normalize data, including de-identifying sensitive information and standardizing measurement units.
- **Analytics and Summarization:**
  Apply a combination of statistical analysis and retrieval-augmented generation (RAG) to generate patient summaries and highlight critical health indicators.
- **Output and Reporting:**
  Present the final reports on an interactive dashboard for healthcare professionals, enabling quick review and informed decisions.

Outcomes:

- Improved accuracy in patient data reporting.
- Faster turnaround times in generating clinical insights.

- Enhanced compliance with data privacy regulations through automated de-identification processes.

Case Study 2: Finance – Automated Risk Assessment and Trading Strategies

Objective:
Develop a multi-agent system that continuously monitors financial markets, assesses risk, and executes trading strategies in real time.

Workflow Overview:

- **Market Data Integration:**
  Ingest real-time financial data, including stock prices, market indices, and economic indicators, via APIs and webhooks.
- **Risk Assessment:**
  Deploy processing agents to analyze market trends and compute risk metrics using statistical models and machine learning algorithms.
- **Decision-Making and Execution:**
  Utilize a decision-making agent to trigger trading strategies based on predefined risk thresholds and market conditions.
- **Feedback and Optimization:**
  Monitor performance through real-time metrics and logs, and incorporate iterative feedback to fine-tune trading algorithms.

Outcomes:

- Increased efficiency in market monitoring and decision-making.
- Reduction in human error and faster reaction times to market fluctuations.
- Improved portfolio performance through dynamic risk-adjusted trading strategies.

Case Study 3: Retail – Personalized Customer Engagement

Objective:
Enhance customer engagement by delivering personalized recommendations and promotions through an intelligent chatbot.

Workflow Overview:

- **User Interaction:**
  Capture customer queries and browsing behavior through a chat interface and website analytics.
- **Content Retrieval and Generation:**
  Use a combination of LLM nodes and RAG systems to generate personalized product recommendations and promotional messages based on customer preferences and historical data.
- **Multi-Agent Coordination:**
  Integrate agents that manage query classification, contextual data retrieval, and response generation to deliver cohesive and engaging customer interactions.
- **Feedback Loop:**
  Collect customer feedback and engagement metrics to continuously refine the personalization algorithms.

Outcomes:

- Increased customer satisfaction through tailored interactions.
- Higher conversion rates driven by relevant recommendations.
- Continuous improvement of the recommendation system based on real-time user feedback.

Case Study 4: Smart Cities – Integrated Traffic Management

Objective:
Implement an intelligent traffic management system that optimizes traffic flow and reduces congestion using real-time sensor data and predictive analytics.

Workflow Overview:

- **Data Collection:**
  Gather real-time data from traffic sensors, cameras, and IoT devices deployed throughout the city.
- **Data Processing and Analytics:**
  Process and analyze the data using agentic workflows to detect congestion patterns, accidents, or roadblocks.
- **Decision-Making and Control:**
  Deploy decision-making agents that adjust traffic signals, provide rerouting suggestions, and communicate with connected vehicles to alleviate congestion.
- **Visualization and Monitoring:**
  Display real-time traffic updates and historical analytics on an interactive dashboard for city traffic managers.

Outcomes:

- Improved traffic flow and reduced congestion during peak hours.
- Enhanced situational awareness for traffic management teams.
- Better resource allocation for emergency response and infrastructure planning.

Use Case: Automated Content Generation for Digital Marketing

Objective:
Streamline the content creation process by automatically generating blog posts, social media updates, and promotional materials based on trending topics and audience insights.

Workflow Overview:

- **Content Input:**
  Capture trending topics and keywords from social media analytics and market research data.
- **LLM-Powered Generation:**
  Utilize LLM nodes to generate initial drafts of content tailored to the specified topics, adjusting tone and style as needed.
- **Editing and Refinement:**
  Implement post-processing nodes to refine and format the content,

ensuring that it meets quality standards and aligns with brand guidelines.
- **Distribution:**
Automatically schedule and distribute the final content through integrated marketing platforms.

Outcomes:

- Reduced content creation time and operational costs.
- Increased engagement through timely and relevant content.
- Continuous improvement of content strategies based on performance analytics.

Summary

Appendix D offers a diverse range of additional case studies and use cases, showcasing how Flowise AI can be applied across industries—from healthcare and finance to retail and smart cities. These examples illustrate the platform's versatility in handling complex, real-world challenges through modular, agentic workflows and advanced integration techniques. By studying these case studies, you can gain valuable insights into best practices and innovative approaches for leveraging Flowise AI in your own projects.

Appendix E: Resources for Further Learning

This appendix provides a curated list of resources to help you deepen your understanding of Flowise AI and the broader field of artificial intelligence. Whether you're looking to enhance your technical skills, explore advanced topics, or engage with the community, the following resources will serve as valuable guides on your learning journey.

Books and Research Papers

- **Foundational AI Texts:**
  - *Deep Learning* by Ian Goodfellow, Yoshua Bengio, and Aaron Courville – A comprehensive introduction to deep learning principles and techniques.

- o *Pattern Recognition and Machine Learning* by Christopher M. Bishop – Offers foundational knowledge in machine learning and statistical techniques.
- **Specialized Topics:**
  - o Research papers on transformer architectures, such as "Attention Is All You Need" – Provides insights into the core innovations behind modern LLMs.
  - o Recent publications on Retrieval-Augmented Generation (RAG) systems and agentic workflows for up-to-date perspectives on emerging trends.

Online Courses and Tutorials

- **MOOCs and Courses:**
  - o Coursera, edX, and Udacity offer courses on deep learning, natural language processing, and AI system design that cover both theoretical and practical aspects.
  - o Specialized courses on platforms like Fast.ai for hands-on training in deep learning and model fine-tuning.
- **Flowise AI Tutorials:**
  - o Look for official Flowise AI tutorials on the platform's website and YouTube channel, which provide step-by-step walkthroughs and real-world examples.
  - o Community-created video tutorials and webinars that demonstrate advanced configurations and integrations.

Documentation and Official Guides

- **Flowise AI Documentation:**
  - o The official Flowise AI documentation provides comprehensive guides on installation, configuration, API usage, and customization. It's an essential reference for both beginners and advanced users.
- **API Reference Manuals:**
  - o Detailed API reference documentation for Flowise AI is available, offering technical details, endpoint descriptions, and sample code to help you integrate and extend the platform.

Community Forums and Developer Platforms

- **Discussion Forums:**
  - Participate in Flowise AI community forums and Q&A sites like Stack Overflow to ask questions, share experiences, and troubleshoot issues.
- **Social Media and Developer Groups:**
  - Engage with community groups on Slack, Discord, LinkedIn, and Reddit where users discuss best practices, feature updates, and innovative use cases.
- **GitHub Repositories:**
  - Explore Flowise AI's official GitHub repository and community-contributed projects. Reviewing code, issues, and pull requests can provide valuable insights into practical applications and customizations.

Blogs, Newsletters, and Conferences

- **Technical Blogs:**
  - Follow blogs from leading AI research labs and companies (e.g., OpenAI, Google AI, DeepMind) for the latest breakthroughs and implementation strategies.
- **Newsletters:**
  - Subscribe to AI newsletters (such as The Batch by deeplearning.ai) and Flowise AI updates to receive regular insights and announcements directly in your inbox.
- **Conferences and Webinars:**
  - Attend AI conferences, workshops, and webinars that cover topics related to Flowise AI, LLMs, and advanced AI workflows. These events provide opportunities for learning and networking with industry experts.

Summary

Appendix E offers a wealth of resources designed to support your continuous learning and professional development in AI and Flowise AI. By exploring books, online courses, official documentation, community forums, and industry events, you can stay updated on the latest trends, deepen your technical expertise, and engage with a vibrant community of practitioners. These resources will not only enhance your understanding of Flowise AI but also empower you to innovate and build more effective AI workflows.

Index

R

- RAG (Retrieval-Augmented Generation) Systems, 5.1–5.4
- Real-Time Logging, 10.2.1

S

- Scalability, 10.4, 8.3
- Security
    - API Security, 7.2
    - Data Protection, 10.3.1

T

- Troubleshooting, 9.3, Appendix C

U

- UI/UX Enhancements, 11.3.1

V

- Version Control, 10.3.1, 10.4

W

- Workflow
    - Definition and Optimization, 1.1, 3.1, 10.1
    - Monitoring and Debugging, 9.3, 10.2, Appendix C

Z

- Zero Downtime Deployment, 9.2

Note: Page numbers and section references are indicative and may vary with the final formatting of the book.